Domestic – adj., pertaining to the home
Commando – n., elite soldier

"This is a great book for parents! This book provides a lot of support, tips and validation for the stay at home parent...all done with a healthy dose of humor to boot!"
- Katy Haney, Publisher
Macaroni Kid, Columbia, Maryland

"She has a passion for helping moms who work at home realize how important their jobs are."
- Kevin & Taylor in the Morning
104.7 The Fish/WFSH-FM Atlanta

"I really enjoyed the tone of this book; my father is retired military and so the author's references to being a commando, feeding the troops on the home front, and strategic principles for tactical operations felt like home to me (the humor is great too!)"
- Anmarie Bowden, Reviewer
SelfhelpMagazine, www.SelfhelpMagazine.com
Marlene M. Maheu, Ph.D., Editor-in-Chief

Domestic Commando's *kitchen tips are practical, easy and very adaptable for first time as well as experienced family cooks."*
- Chef Jewels Quelly
Contours Food Segment Host
91.9 FM, Public Radio from Centenary College, Hackettstown, NJ

"This book is so full of practical tips that parents can use every single day. Yet, it was Toni's suggestion to create an Heirloom Box for my family that really spoke to my heart. It's such a wonderful idea!"
- Sherry Tatum, co-host
Friends & Neighbors, Syndicated television series

"I love this book! Humor is my life, even more so as a new mom. I love the way the book is written. Having great tips and tactics to make life run a little more smoothly is just a great bonus."
- Amy Lundy Lusthaus, owner
small fry society and bun in the oven bunch, Tampa, Fl

When you work from home, are you called a stay-at-home writer, a stay-at-home businessman, or a stay-at-home radiologist? Domestic Commando *is long overdue.*
- Dahlia Kurtz
Writer/Columnist

DOMESTIC COMMANDO

A Stay-at-Home (R)evolution

TONI GARCIA CARPENTER

Wolf Creek Publishing, LLC

ISBN: 0982161220
ISBN-13: 9780982161227
Library of Congress Control Number: 2010913474

Published by Wolf Creek Publishing, LLC
Jacksonville, Florida, USA
info@WolfCreekPublishing.com

Website
DomesticCommando.com

Printed in the United States of America

To Hub.b

Autofocus!
How lucky are we that we still laugh
together after all these years?

To G2 and Tweets

You are the reasons I always wanted to do my best.
But the truth is, the two of you are my best work.
"3"

TABLE OF CONTENTS

PREFACE

Since you're reading this book, you may at least suspect that you are a Domestic Commando. It's important to realize that one of the fundamental principles of being a Domestic Commando is that, in a time when a salaried career is the standard of success, you have elected to take the time to raise your child yourself and to strive to do an exceptional job.

Frankly, you don't care what tune the rest of the band is playing; your song is marked by a completely different rhythm. This can make for a pretty lonely solo performance some days.

In the following pages, I hope to reveal that there are others who hear that same rhythm and tackle this career with the same zeal that a salaried employee would (or should).

I begin with Boot Camp: the essentials of being a Domestic Commando. Our training doesn't involve obstacle courses or five-mile slogs. It's about attitude, self-respect and commitment.

Next are Strategic Principles and Tactical Operations. Strategy addresses the long-term, big picture while tactics are the tips and tricks I have found to help me achieve little day-to-day victories on the front lines.

Ready Packs come in two varieties: essential and helpful. They are the tools that help me ensure my family's best interests in an emergency and help me to be efficient and organized.

Feeding the Troops is, hopefully, an inspirational chapter of tips and easy recipes that have been mainstays in our family. I have even included a couple of the "weirder" recipes for your amusement, and to confirm that every family has its own quirks.

Throughout the book, I have dropped in some *Tales from the Trenches*—anecdotal stories of my personal experiences as a Domestic

Commando. While they are not likely to be universal experiences, they may elicit an "aha" moment, or at least a knowing nod. I believe most Domestic Commandos will find some comfort, perspective, and hopefully even a little humor in these tales.

Generally, the pronouns "he" and "she" are used alternately within the text to keep the sentences less cumbersome as there is no gender-neutral pronoun for an individual.

I've purposely kept most of my comments fairly brief because Domestic Commandos rarely have large blocks of free time. I hope you will regularly enlist the use of this handbook for tips, tricks and perspective as you pursue your own Domestic Commando (r)evolution.

DISCLAIMER

Raising a child is the responsibility of that child's parents. Nothing in this book should be considered medical or professional advice. You should always check with your medical professional if you have any questions or concerns about your child.

ACKNOWLEDGEMENTS

I would be remiss if I didn't take a moment to thank some of the wonderful people who have supported my efforts to create *Domestic Commando*.

My daughter, Kate, was always the first to read the book, in all its permutations, and helped confirm that I remembered things correctly. I was especially grateful that she laughed in all the right places.

My dad, Anthony Garcia, never asked questions and never discouraged me from accomplishing my goal. That's just his style.

My sister, Valerie Hubbell, was always enthusiastic and encouraging. A true Domestic-Commando-at-heart, she also is the recipient of our family's crafting gene.

I am extremely grateful to Christa Aldinger (homeschooling mother of three) and Alison Worret (mother of four boys) for taking time to read the manuscript and forward their comments. They are remarkable women who are "kinda busy," as Alison likes to say.

My sister-in-law, Sharon Maddux Carpenter, was the motivation for writing our first book, *The Hurricane Handbook*. With one published book under my belt, I had the confidence to write this one. More importantly, her knowledge, talent and heart as an early childhood educator and coach made her the most wonderful sounding board while I was raising my kids.

Finally, I am delighted to have had the opportunity to work with artist Nick Wolensky. He took the sad little sketch I emailed him (I truly cannot draw) and combined it with some basic suggestions and information and created "Just Ducky," my mascot-logo. It was just what I was looking for, and Nick definitely has a spot in the "Call First" section of my card file.

BOOT CAMP

It's an Attitude

THE DOMESTIC COMMANDO MISSION

The Domestic Commando way of life is about raising our families to the best of our abilities while rejecting the stigma attached to the decision to stay at home. In other words, this is about attitude...and attitude adjustment.

Most of us are moms, but there are some dads out there, too. Regardless, as Domestic Commandos, we are confident in, and proud of, the work we do. Anyone who chooses to demean our work simply needs to adjust his or her own attitude...or be dismissed as irrelevant. We are adamant that our path deserves no less respect than any other.

Period!

Conversely, Domestic Commandos don't pass judgment on the paths others choose—or need—to take. There are likely many Domestic-Commandos-at-heart who realistically have no other option than to work outside the home. They deserve our support.

We have the oldest, toughest, most influential career there is. Our decisions and our actions affect the health and happiness of those within our theater of operations...just like a four-star general's do.

Of course, we're just operating on a smaller scale with a much more challenging budget!

THE MAKING OF
A DOMESTIC COMMANDO

It was shortly before my firstborn turned one that I assumed the title *Domestic Commando*.

I had struggled with my "identity" since the day he was born: *Who am I...or, should I ask, what am I?*

To put this in perspective, let me introduce myself. I'm Toni Garcia Carpenter. I have a degree in broadcast production with a combined minor in chemistry and mathematics. I worked in communications, both in a newsroom and in corporate public relations, until I became pregnant with my first child.

At seven months pregnant, I was one of a slew of managers laid off at our company for economic reasons. I was lucky enough to have the option to stay home with my child after he was born. And that was what I did.

In fact, that is what I had been secretly hoping for. From the moment I confirmed I was pregnant, my heart's desire was to stay home with my child.

Yet, I was totally unprepared for this new career. There was no leaving work at five or even six. I *lived* at the "office." Working late took on a whole new meaning: chronic sleep deprivation.

And then there was the "boss." "I'm hungry...WAH!" "My diaper needs changing...WAH!" "I'm tired...WAH, WAH, WAH!" I'd never had such a demanding boss.

Nor a more appreciative one. I'd give anything to see that gummy smile.

I loved my job.

And then it happened—my first "grown up" social event without the baby. I couldn't wait for real conversation! You know, when you talk, and the other person can actually respond with words! I looked forward to it all week.

I think it took all of five minutes. Still nursing, I was getting a soda from the bar when the person next to me asked, "So what do you do?"

"I'm home with my baby."

Ka-Blam! I had committed the equivalent of social suicide.

Without a word, the party-goer turned and walked away. I'm not kidding! Apparently, if I didn't have a "job," I must be uninteresting and probably not very smart.

If I hadn't been so angry, I would have been hurt. Clearly, this dolt didn't have a clue about the many skills it takes to stay home. I was juggling the jobs of accountant, caretaker, chef, courier, health-care provider, playmate, teacher, office manager, housekeeper, and gardener. I was managing all the little tasks of making our household run smoothly with the added responsibility of caring for a helpless baby—and doing a fine job of it, thank you very much!

The problem was that there wasn't an adequate or satisfactory job title to express what millions of other people and I were tasked with— *and accomplished*—every day.

"Stay-at-home-mom" was simply inaccurate. I spent entirely too much time running errands to imply I was at home all that much. Not to mention, it just sounded so…*passive.* It didn't even begin to reflect the amount of work involved or the enthusiasm I had for the job.

Then there was the term "housewife." I married a man, not a house. (I'm sure that marrying a building would be considered an unnatural act in many states. At least, it should be). So, no, I wasn't a housewife.

I struggled with my identity crisis for almost a year until, one morning, the answer came by way of a television commercial. You remember the one for the U.S. Army? "We do more by 9:00 a.m. than most people do all day."

That was it!

The morning had barely begun and I had already given my son his morning bottle, made breakfast, cleaned the kitchen (at least twice), started my second load of laundry, put my son down for a nap, dusted the house and was getting ready to fit in some exercise before vacuuming and cleaning the bathrooms.

When I was working "in the world" I would just be finishing the morning paper by this time.

It was in that moment of clarity that I realized I wasn't a housewife, or a stay-at-home-mom, or any other milquetoast appellation. I was a *Domestic Commando.*

Hoo ya! This breakthrough was the first step in my personal (r)evolution. Every day and month that passed, I evolved into a more confident, productive parent while revolting against the judgment of others.

If society is so compelled to label me, then *I* shall choose the label that suits me.

When you call yourself a Domestic Commando, you acknowledge how important your work is, how hard you work, and how competent you are. As our longtime family friend Phyllis noted, "We *are* in command!" With this comes the attitude. It's important to understand that this is not about lifestyle; this is about attitude. If I have to explain this, you're probably not a Domestic Commando.

Being a Domestic Commando also simplifies social exchanges. Next time someone asks you what you do, tell them you're a Domestic Commando. With your education, investment, compassion, and ingenuity, there is simply no one better suited or more qualified to raise your child than you are.

You're not likely to be dismissed as uninteresting. Scary, maybe—but certainly not dull.

And *that* is very satisfying, indeed!

THINGS HAVE CHANGED

It's comforting to consider a little historical perspective.

For a variety of reasons, today's Domestic Commandos often don't have the built-in support that was common just a couple of generations ago.

Rarely do we live in the towns and communities we grew up in. The people who would normally step in to give us a break and take care of a teething baby often live hundreds or even thousands of miles away. Extended families have given way to nuclear families and even sub-nuclear families (with single heads of households).

Then there's the suburb factor. Suburbs have been built to provide an escape from the congestion of the city. But suburbs are *new* neighborhoods drawing *new* families. Rarely do you move in knowing the people living near you.

There's no corner market to deliver your groceries.

The comfort and luxury of a built-in support system are gone. Few of us experience the real-life education that comes from watching generations grow up around us.

Education is focused on getting a job or beginning a career.

Then, one day, someone hands us a newborn like we're supposed to know what to do with it.

Go figure.

RE-EDUCATION

I spent seven years in college.

I liked college. I learned lots of stuff in college. I learned how to be *a job title* (writer/producer), to be self-sufficient, to earn a living. I felt confident to tackle any job I went after.

My confidence exploded into the ether like the helium in an over-inflated balloon the moment they handed me my first child.

Excuse me! Now what? Where's the textbook? How about a class syllabus? Maybe we could go home with you and arrange a limited internship program. I'm a quick study...18 years should do it.

I was clueless.

I was handed the biggest responsibility of my life, and no formal education to go with it. So what was left?

Analysis and instinct.

I knew I could observe and analyze. Those were skills I had learned to do in school. So I thoughtfully analyzed all the advice I had received and all the books and magazine articles I could read.

On the other hand, I felt instinct had merit, as well. After all, most animals parent through instinct. But instinct was much harder to embrace because of my training to analyze. Analysis can block instinct because it leads to "over-thinking."

Often, I found myself analyzing information simply to determine what *made sense*...and this was often what simply *felt right*. And that is how I learned to parent.

Sometimes I missed the mark completely. Other times I discovered that what had worked for one child didn't always work for the other.

But until they start handing out manuals, I firmly believe we get points for trying our best.

MOMMY BRAIN

Researchers have determined that after we give birth, we have difficulty thinking and remembering.

Apparently, "mommy brain," as my sister-in-law and I call it, is the result of evil hormones bouncing around in our systems.

I thought it was the result of going several months without making it through one complete sleep cycle.

But that's just me.

CRISIS MANAGEMENT

You never know when your child's fragile world will be upended by a crisis.

Whether the situation is due to a falling out with a best friend or the crushing experience of not being picked for the team, you will be your child's principal source of comfort. Here are some general guidelines that have worked for me.

For a young child:
1. Listen.
2. Offer perspective.
3. Console (as needed.)
4. Hug generously.

For a teenager (*some* scenarios)
1. See above.

For a teenager (all other scenarios)
1. Suggest.
2. Cajole.
3. Scream. (He or she may have slept through 1 and 2.)
4. Threaten.
5. Take yourself to a movie.
6. Hit stash of dark chocolate.

In all cases:
Pray often and pray hard.

JUST DUCKY!

As Domestic Commandos, we take pride in having our act together. It's just part of who we are. Unfortunately, real life doesn't always cooperate, and we may have to "fake it 'til we make it" in order to *appear* as if we've got things under control.

I take my inspiration from ducks. They float serenely on the water, never revealing how madly they may be paddling just below the surface to overcome an adverse current.

Although the idea that we should never let them see us sweat is directed to the outside world, it does boost our self-confidence when we gracefully get through a tough patch.

No single item is more important to the goal of never letting them see you sweat than the battle dress uniform (BDU).

Let me set the stage.

It's 6:52 a.m.

Normally you'd be up and proceeding with the morning routine. On this particular morning, you are just closing your eyes. The night has been spent nursing a pitiful child who's been <u>insert word(s)</u> (feverish, vomiting, itching, teething, ouchy, etc.).

Your eyelids are heavy enough to use as weights for bicep curls. Stringing together more than four or five words is almost impossible (unless general babbling is acceptable...which it isn't) and you suspect you smell bad.

But your trials are not over.

Just as sleep washes over you...the doorbell rings. It's the appliance repairman! It took days, maybe weeks, to get this appointment. Worse yet, you may be charged a cancellation fee. There's no choice but to answer the door.

Of course, you could shuffle to the door in your robe and mumble some excuse about a sick kid. But as a Domestic Commando, you've set a higher bar for yourself. It's time to rely on preparation and strategy.

Step 1: The BDU. You should *always* have at least one outfit on hand that slips on in just a couple of seconds. The color(s) should make you feel good and should be bright enough to make you appear awake. Keep your uniform handy (and clean) on a hook where you can reach for it in an emergency. (My favorite was a knit dress with a drop waist that slipped right over my head with no buttons or zippers. It sported large, impressionist-style flowers. The pattern camouflaged almost every stain my kids and I could throw at it. I actually wore the dress out).

Step 2: Grooming. Run your fingers through your hair (this will confirm that there's no leftover puke in it—if so, grab a scarf or sacrificial head band). As you walk to the door, a stroke of tinted lip gloss is a nice touch (lipstick requires too much coordination right now). Keep a favorite gloss on the bathroom counter or in a drawer near the entryway of your home, preferably near a mirror.

Step 3: Speech. Babbling is a dead giveaway. So stick to a script. Never speak more than three words at a time and remember to smile. It makes your words sound more energetic.
  "Be right there!"
  "Hi." or *"Good morning!"*
  "Thanks for coming."
  "Right this way."
Draw on your adrenaline to briefly answer questions about whatever it is that brought this person to your home.

Step 4: The vigil. Make yourself something to drink, offering some to service person.

"Coffee?"
"Tea?"
"Orange juice?"
"Juice box?"
"Red Bull?"

Step 5: Sit in front of the TV and use the time to remember where you put your purse, so you you'll be ready to pay the bill. *Do not read.* Your head may fall into the book—totally humiliating. Do not do chores. You've earned some comp time for the night shift. You'll catch up later.

Step 6: Pay quickly. Escort service person to the door. Walk briskly to bed. Fall in.

Step 7: Retrieve whimpering child who has just woken up. Provide appropriate sustenance.

Step 8: Call spouse. Declare home a no-fly zone and/or under quarantine. Turn off phones. Sleep whenever child does for the next thirty-six hours.

SEASONS

Throughout the years I've been asked by friends and acquaintances, who knew me as *the* Domestic Commando, when I was going to get around to writing about it.

I would always answer, "Soon." *Soon* took more than ten years!

At times I wondered why procrastination on this issue was such a challenge for me. I told myself that I was simply busy with whatever was going on in my life at the time; too busy to write a book. Later, when my kids started going to school full time, I returned to the workforce on a freelance basis and thought it would be hypocritical to write about being a Domestic Commando. I suffered something of a writer's block on the subject, and the idea went dormant.

I have always been a relatively prolific writer. During my children's nap times and in the early morning hours I co-wrote a book on hurricane preparedness for families. When my kids got older, I wrote scripts for several lifestyle television shows before expanding into producing and directing, making use of my degree. As a writer, I have always believed there was no such thing as writer's block. If a writing project came to a grinding halt, it just meant that there was a piece of information missing. I simply needed to return to my research to find the missing piece—that bit of truth that makes everything come together.

What I was missing in regard to the Domestic Commando book concept wasn't information that had been previously hidden or overlooked. After all, this was about *my* attitude and experiences. What was missing was perspective. That perspective came in the form of a revelation that clarified my (r)evolution. Here it is:

My life isn't one long string of events that come one right after the other, in a cascade of moments that blur by, and will end when I finally take my last breath. My life is a series of seasons, one flowing naturally into the next, often marked by some rite of passage.

As I mused on this revelation of seasons, events from my life fell into place within the bigger picture.

First, there was the season of my childhood: schoolwork and playtime molded my days.

With my high school diploma in hand, I moved on to college: the season in which I learned a profession and self-reliance.

When I graduated, I began a season in which I learned some of the ropes of the work place.

At age thirty, when I had my first child, my season as a full-time Domestic Commando began. I was very lucky because my husband and I were able to live without my income for a time, and we agreed that this was what we wanted.

The transition to the next season took several years, which makes it something of a season all its own. As each child started pre-kindergarten, I had more time to pursue other endeavors. In my case, I chose to write. I am a morning person, and prefer to write then, so the Pre-K schedule was perfect for me.

At the same time, it was during this season that I became conflicted about being a Domestic Commando. I actually felt guilty because my free time wasn't being spent volunteering every day at the children's school, or baking cookies every single day for after-school treats. I got over it when I paid off my student loans with the money I made writing while my kids were in class.

Roger that!

Domestic Commandos are practical above all else.

As my kids have grown and have become more self-sufficient, I have been able to do more, as well. Yes, my seasons have evolved in response to my children's needs. But there's nothing wrong with that: It's part of the life I have chosen!

The bottom line is simple: If you choose to have children, you are no longer a single entity. There is a synergy that occurs when you become a parent. Your life is inextricably intertwined with the lives of those in your family. The seasons of their lives will affect the seasons of your life, and vice versa.

It was important for me to understand this, and it's important for any Domestic Commando to realize this. Why? Because new seasons lie ahead: resuming your career, picking a different job altogether, or remaining a full-time Domestic Commando with more time for yourself. (This is not a crime and should not be treated as one—the rest of the world should just get over it).

Seasons change, and sometimes this understanding is what gets me through the day. Whatever the challenge of the day is, I know that it won't last forever. There is always a new season coming. And when it arrives, I just might find that it came a little too soon.

Very simply, I have learned to be grateful for each season I have the privilege to experience.

$CHA-CHING$

Let me address the elephant in the room.

Because we've chosen to be Domestic Commandos, our families do not have the "benefit" of a second income.

Of course, how much that income would ultimately provide is subject to debate. By the time you account for the price of day care, work wardrobe, fuel, restaurant lunches and a higher, combined tax bracket, you may not be "making" as much as you thought.

Nonetheless, in this day of unrealistic (i.e. ludicrous) material expectations, it is too easy for any family to spend its way into debt. For decades, the rule has been to build your credit score. Of course, the only way to do that is to buy on credit. We now know how devastating that mindset is.

I am not a money wizard, but I have found a couple of books that I wish had been available to me sooner.

For big picture, take-care-of-your-family information, I really like Suze Ormon's *9 Steps to Financial Freedom*. She explains the intricacies of everything from wills and trusts to medical directives in a way that I could finally understand.

But for a no-nonsense, get-out-of-debt/stay-out-of-debt approach to money, I love Dave Ramsey's, take-no-prisoners approach. His *Total Money Makeover* is a straightforward, easy read and has just the attitude to which a Domestic Commando can relate. Many of the success stories he shares in his book are from single-income families who prove it can be done.

Getting out of debt and being out of debt is the ultimate freedom, and the best example we can set for our children. It means we have to buck the trends and the pressures to conform to social norms. But as Domestic Commandos, we're already miles ahead in that race!

THE JUST-RIGHT ATTITUDE

We could learn a lot from a fairy tale.

Remember Goldilocks and how she judged many things to be too hard or too soft, too hot or too cold, too big or too small? What seemed to be the story of a very fussy person was really a study in moderation. She always found something in between the two extremes to be "just right."

This is an excellent attitude for a Domestic Commando. Let's start with something big and obvious. Home. There's an excellent series of books by Sarah Susanka that introduces the "not-so-big house" concept. It encourages homeowners to reconsider the oversized, myriad-roomed mini mansion with the high ceilings in favor of a manageable home on a more human scale. Admit it: It's hard to feel cozy in a room with an echo.

Then there's the issue of acquisitions.

Do we really need every new appliance out there? Is it truly necessary to wear the absolute latest fashion? (And whose idea of fashion is it, anyway?) How big does a car have to be before it's too big (and too annoying to park and too expensive to operate)?

To break the current culture of "Bigger is Best! and More is Better!" we first need to adopt the just-right attitude. We must begin by carefully considering what we *really* need. What is just right for our families? With this information firmly in mind, we're able to make choices we can really live with.

For example, our home was built in the 1950s. The traditional layout was not always the most functional. A couple of years ago, we looked into adding on to address some of these problems: I wanted a dedicated utility room and more storage; the family room was long and narrow and lacked adequate wall space. With only two bathrooms, guests had to use the hall bathroom, which was the kids' bathroom. (There's no need to go into additional detail here. You know the issues involved.)

Our home is almost 2,400 square feet. The addition was going to increase it by about 1,400 square feet, and we were going to gain a "public" bathroom, which guests could use without donning hazmat suits. Finally!

But the more I thought about it, the *less* I liked the idea. It was going to be a lot more house to dust, a third bathroom to disinfect, and 1,400 more square feet of floor to clean. I hate vacuuming and mopping (even though I love the results when I'm done!). What was I thinking? So we re-evaluated what we really needed and took a careful look at what we had to work with.

For significantly less money, my husband and I reworked a small, multi-purpose room next to the kitchen. We had a plumber move the pipes for the washing machine; we put up new drywall; and, together in two days, we assembled and mounted fourteen new cabinets that we ordered from a home improvement store. It was fun, productive, and gave us a very useful room. We had someone come in to update the hall bath for us, and we even built a deck that we absolutely love outside our family room.

And all for a fraction of the money it would have cost us to add on.

That really made it "just right."

VALIDATION

A Tale from the Trenches

The experience was almost surreal.

I had volunteered for field-trip duty. This field trip was to be a cultural experience held in the theater at the local state university. I don't remember all the details because it took place so many years ago, yet it changed many of my views about my place in the world.

The cultural presentation was a performance of African music, primarily percussion and rhythm. The musicians were a family: father, mother, grown daughters and the third-generation that came onto the stage, as well. Some were old enough to participate in the performance, others were definitely too small.

Prior to playing each piece, the father, in a voice rich with the lilting cadence of his culture, would explain something about the music or the instruments to the very attentive audience.

I noticed that none of the adults on stage moved in a hurried manner. In fact, their movements were as elegant as their speech. I couldn't help but notice that the children on stage were very comfortable and calm.

Then, toward the end of the performance, the youngest child, a baby who had been asleep at his mother's feet during the entire performance, began to fuss. His mother simply picked him up, set him onto one of the beautiful pieces of fabric that she'd been wearing draped over her shoulders, and in one exquisite, fluid movement, tied him piggyback onto her body.

Matter-of-factly—and frankly, with some pride—the father explained that, in his country, *this* is what they call day care.

Hoo ya! I was elated.

It was my first experience with external validation of my decision to raise my children myself by being home with them during the day. It had come from a man with a lilting voice, representing an ancient culture and heritage.

It seemed strange, and almost a little sad, that I related so well to people of another country and culture. But I now realize that certain decisions and attitudes are more universal in nature and transcend cultural and political boundaries.

I will be forever grateful to the patriarch of that beautiful family for boosting my self-esteem with his comments that day.

PRICELESS

Every year or so, there's an article or a news story about what stay-at-home moms would be earning in the "real world."

I don't bother to read them.

As my friend, and ultra-Domestic Commando Christa adamantly points out, Domestic Commandos "are a vital link of what is good and right and a necessary part of a well rounded, functioning community."

At home, I know that I am chef, housekeeper, bookkeeper, lawn service, taxi driver, interior designer, personal shopper, laundry service, nutritionist, party planner, photographer, etc. Each of these would provide an adequate salary, and the overtime compensation alone would break the back of most companies.

But how do you put a price on my role as reading buddy, on-call nurse, tickle monster, teacher, family historian, advocate, and safe zone? You can't.

Anyone who believes his worth is measured in dollars should probably be pitied.

I don't need anyone to put a dollar figure on my value.

PERSPECTIVE

Being a Domestic Commando isn't about living a life of domestic perfection.

Day-to-day life is about being efficient and effective and doing the best job we can for our families and for ourselves. But let's face it. Some days, it's a challenge just to make it to the end of the day.

The big picture can be overwhelming. We've got these precious lives entrusted to us, and we can't always count on the cavalry showing up to bail us out when we're faced with the inevitable challenges of real life.

But we have to put it into perspective. This is a long-term endeavor, and we have signed on for the duration. Never lose sight that the ultimate measure of our success is whether, in the end, we've raised happy, healthy, decent human beings.

STRATEGIC PRINCIPLES

The Big Picture

A PERSONAL PRINCIPLE

I have never bothered with regrets.

The way I see it, I've always tried to carefully gather the best information available before making a decision. If circumstances later changed, how could I have known that would happen? My intentions were good and I made the best choices I could with the information I had at the time.

If anyone faults me for that, she simply does not need to be a part of my life. She is free to take her judgment — and wallow in it — somewhere else.

I make no apologies.

BABY MAMA

I just love ten-month old babies.

Their needs are still simple: They need to eat, to sleep, and to be cleaned. They will sit (for a short while) to be read to. They can play simple games. (How big is baby? SO BIG!) They giggle and cuddle and are absolutely delicious! I was meant to be a mom to babies.

But one day, a terrible thing happens: The babies learn to talk back.

And when that occurs, I must assume the mantle of the parentally challenged.

I just ignore what I can; holler about what I must; and know that one day, the babies will have babies. And when those babies learn to talk back, I'll gleefully return them to their parents.

Maybe the great "circle of life" is really payback!

TWERP (A EUPHEMISM)

A Tale from the Trenches

When my firstborn was six months old, we moved back to Florida from the northern Virginia suburbs. The stress of moving didn't compare to the challenge of finding a new pediatrician. I loved my old pediatricians. They were mature, Cuban-born gentlemen with a world of knowledge about kids ... a brilliant combination of education and good, old, common sense. I knew my child was in good hands.

By the time we moved, we weren't due for another well-baby checkup for two months. I don't remember to whom we went, but he or she simply wasn't right for us. So I now had another two months to continue searching for a new pediatrician.

Eventually, an acquaintance recommended a young, thriving practice. She raved about them. They were up on all the latest information, and so on.

I called to make an appointment for the ten-month-old well-baby checkup. Because this was such a busy practice, they actually weren't able to schedule us right away. We ended up with an appointment that was essentially a ten-and-a-half-month-old well-baby checkup.

We arrived on time at the tidy new office. The nurse handled the usual weighing, measuring, and questioning, and then she left. She was later replaced by a tall doctor in his late twenties or early thirties. I suspected he was too young to be a parent.

The doctor followed the typical baby review: throat, ears, chest. It was unremarkable until he asked "the question." That's when everything changed.

"Has he taken his first step?"

"Oh, he's walking," I replied matter-of-factly.

(I must take a moment to explain that I'm one of those people who believes that different children focus on different things at different times. For some, it's walking early, for others it's expanding verbal skills, and others concentrate on refining eye-hand coordination. Whether my child walked early was not a particularly big deal, it was simply a fact).

"Really?" he replied, his voice skeptical. "Show me."

Slightly annoyed, I lifted my son from the examining table, stood him on the floor, walked back a few steps, and encouraged him to "Come to Mommy."

He toddled over, I picked him up and propped him on my hip. I didn't say a word, thinking, *Ball's in your court, Twerp!*

The volley was devastating!

"Is he on the cup yet?"

A bottle, filled with formula, was in full view.

"No," I replied.

"Well, all our babies are off the bottle at one year," he announced sternly. He looked at the chart. "So you have six weeks."

He may as well have called me a negligent mother!

I tried to run through the reasons for overlooking this milestone. Bottles were efficient. They weren't messy. Most importantly, my child loved his bottle! I wasn't sure I'd ever even offered my child a cup to drink from. How was I going to accomplish this feat by the deadline that ticked closer every minute? My mind was racing.

Believe it or not, by the time I'd filled out the check for my insurance co-pay and walked out the front door of the office, I had concluded that I had failed my son. I fell into a deep-blue funk (no other way to describe it) and couldn't even tell my family about the baby's checkup.

As luck would have it, the next day we were at a family gathering for some of my husband's long-time friends. I was chatting with one of the other moms and mentioned the experience. I told her how terrible I felt. I guess I figured that if she also concluded that I was a negligent mother, I could simply make excuses for the rest of my life so that I'd never see these folks again. But I had to confess my sin to somebody!

She brushed it off, explaining, "All kids are different! Sometimes a bottle is just what they need. When my child was two, she fell and hurt herself and was miserable. I found a bottle sitting in the cupboard, filled it with milk, and gave it to her. It helped to settle her down."

I looked out at her child: active, healthy, well-adjusted, normal.

I looked at my child: active, healthy, well-adjusted, normal. In fact, as I watched him toddle around with the other kids, you could say he was thriving!

Over and over, I would read the term, "failure to thrive," in the baby books. Clearly that was not my child's problem. He was robust and happy. And that's the bottom line.

My goal, as a Domestic Commando, was and is, to raise a child who is thriving *in his or her own way.* Children shouldn't be expected to reach certain milestones according to someone else's calendar.

So, I got over it—in a big way.

I decided to offer both a bottle and a cup (with a small amount of liquid to minimize the mess) at meals. This way, my child could experiment with the cup and master it at his own pace without the trauma of going cold turkey.

By sixteen months, the bottle was history and cups ruled the dishwasher.

Of course, we never went back to that pediatrician, although I am grateful that the whole experience cemented my confidence as a mom.

Twerp!

MYTH BUSTING

No child ever died of boredom.

However, more than one adult has gone crazy listening to a child whine about dying of boredom.

Kids are being led by the nose to believe that we must provide for their entertainment 24/7. I don't know exactly who wants them to believe this, but we must resist this nonsense.

I have come to realize that boredom has a purpose. It encourages kids to explore, to fill the time with some activity of their own creation, or even just to sit and think.

Of course, the key is to quietly guide them to these opportunities. A basketball hoop or play structures in the yard or a park, a porch swing, a sketch pad and colored pencils, a bicycle, a basket of seasonal books, a picnic blanket, a sand box, a window seat, and so on.

Imagine. Most of these items are affordable and not one of them has a plug, ear buds, or needs to be charged.

IF IT'S TUESDAY, IT MUST BE DANCE CLASS

For some inexplicable reason, over-scheduling has become an acceptable SCD (socially correct disease).

I'm talking about families who need a color-coded, multi-layer calendar to schedule the week's activities. They coordinate practices and rehearsals and classes with the skill of a battalion commander, only to find they have no time for family meals.

If your mini-van or SUV smells perpetually of French fries and your kitchen hasn't smelled like food since the last holiday…STOP!

If the only way you can tell the day of the week is by the obligation to which you are currently driving, you need to get a life so that your family can have one, too.

I admit that I've learned many of my strategic ops through on-the-job training, but this is one procedure that I've practiced from the beginning. I have limited outside activities to no more than two per week. Furthermore, the activity could not disrupt the primary family routine: Family meals eaten together and reasonable bedtimes were not negotiable.

This has been easier for me than for most because Firstborn really wasn't interested in extra activities. But Second-born would be delighted if something were planned eight days a week.

Fortunately, by the time I had to face the predicament of over scheduling, I was sufficiently confident as a Domestic Commando to know that I wasn't going to be shamed into it. I simply was not going to ride around all week with hoop-eyed, exhausted children in order to fulfill someone else's misguided "supermom" ideal.

OUCHY DAYS

It is a phenomenon that I haven't read about anywhere, but nonetheless it is quite real.

You wake up in the morning to find your child is out of sorts. The child is physically healthy—no fever, no rashes, no bumps or bruises, tummy's fine—but he or she is just miserable.

My mother-in-law had a name for it. It was an "ouchy day." The best I can figure is that it's a child's unconscious way of signaling the need for a mental health day.

Ouchy days need to be quiet days. Any planned activity needs to be re-scheduled. This is a day to stay at home, read, snuggle, eat comfort foods, nap. Your child may be grumpy the whole time and may not even seem to appreciate what you're doing.

But imagine if you weren't there.

This is one of the reasons you have chosen to be a Domestic Commando. You are still that child's safety net: the one person who understands that the best way to get through an ouchy day is with loving arms around you.

Of course, an ouchy day that lasts for more than a day should probably signal a trip to the pediatrician.

Generally speaking, the way we as parents respond to ouchy days helps set the tone for how our children remember their childhoods.

THE FIRST BIRTHDAY

A Tale from the Trenches

My firstborn's first birthday was a real celebration. But not for the reasons you might think.

Sure it was a milestone for Baby; but it was also a milestone for me. While guests were urging my child to demolish the beautiful birthday cake placed before him, I was quietly enjoying a celebration of my own.

I was marking *one whole year* that I had managed to take care of my child without screwing up too badly. He was healthy. He was happy. Despite my ignorance of parenting I'd managed *not* to maim or cause him harm through these twelve months — his first year — the year he was most vulnerable. I felt extremely successful. I was virtually giddy with accomplishment. One year down, a lifetime to go!

A daunting thought. But I was already learning: Take it one month, one day, one hour, five minutes at a time. Break it down to manageable elements.

When my kids became teenagers I reminded myself on a daily basis that "This, too, shall pass."

RHYTHM OR BLUES

I love routine.

Let me begin by explaining that routine is not the same as over-scheduling (see *If It's Tuesday, It Must Be Dance Class*). It is, in fact, quite the opposite. Over-scheduling requires a calendar to keep track of where we're supposed to be or what we are supposed to be doing at any given time. It occurs in response to *outside* influences. On the other hand, routine develops *naturally*. It is the pattern of the day that evolves from normal rhythms.

When is nap time? Reading time and calm activities fit naturally before naptime. Busy playtime sensibly takes place after children are rested.

How long is reasonable for a little one to go between meals? I once had a toddler dissolve into a pitiful puddle in the kitchen doorway when the evening meal—normally served at 5:00 p.m.—still had not been served by 5:15.

When I gave it some thought, I realized that little bodies are doing amazing work as they grow and develop. They can only go so long before they must be nourished. I didn't believe in an endless barrage of snacks, so in my home mealtimes had to be as consistent as sleep times. (In homes where there is constant grazing, I've noticed that mealtimes are often more flexible).

So I learned the discipline—and strategy—of a daily routine. This helped me feel in control of my day and gave my young children a feeling of security. I seldom deviated from the routine even though I was considered too inflexible and insufficiently spontaneous as a result. I knew there would be plenty of time for flexibility as the kids got older and routine would revolve around school schedules.

Eventually, unpredictable and excessive teenage sleep habits made an inclusive family routine almost impossible. That's when I found that my planning once again revolved around meals. Feeding on demand was fine when I was nursing, but that was where I drew the line. Mealtimes were announced with the understanding that there were two kinds of people: the quick and the hungry.

Teenagers do not like to be hungry.

CUDDLE ON THE COUCH

Reading with my children was an almost magical experience. It was a treasured part of our daily routine well into grade school. Every evening, after dinner and baths, we would sit on the couch for reading time. It was the perfect way to wind down the day.

Our favorite books were kept handy in a beautiful basket my mother-in-law had woven years earlier. Each child would pick out a couple of books. With one child snuggled on either side of me, I read to them. Many of our favorites were the classic books of childhood:

- Goodnight Moon
- The City Mouse and The Country Mouse (a beautifully illustrated chunky board book)
- The Carl Books
- If You Give a Moose a Muffin / If You Give a Mouse a Cookie
- Dr. Seuss Books
- Cloudy with a Chance of Meatballs
- Where the Wild Things Are

Many books were read so many times that they looked very "loved." We didn't care.

While we always turned to our favorite books to read, I also would rotate in some "seasonal" books that celebrated the time of year or upcoming holidays. I would seek out age-appropriate books that helped tell the story of the season or the celebration. When the season had passed, these books were then stored until the following year to be welcomed like old friends.

While mealtime routines nourished our bodies, reading time nourished us as a family.

MULTITASKING

Multitasking is highly overrated.

I can just imagine the shouts of "Blasphemy!" from all you multitasking Domestic Commandos right now. Better sit down. I'm not finished.

Multitasking is not only overrated, it's just plain wrong.

Take a deep breath while I walk you through this.

My sister-in-law, Sharon, used to call it "plate-spinning." In the hey-day of television variety shows, there regularly appeared some harried soul whose talent was spinning plates on poles. He'd get one plate started, and then another, and another until there was a multitude of poles with plates spinning on top of them.

And then one of the poles would start to wobble, and the plate spinning on top would teeter, and our harried talent would run over to start the plate spinning faster again. But while this plate was being saved, another would begin to teeter, and another, until the spinner was just a panting blur running from one plate to another, trying to keep them all going.

That's what a lot of days are like for a Domestic Commando. Doctor appointments, grocery shopping, making meals, cleaning the kitchen (again), cleaning the house (did I ever stop?), birthday parties, paying bills, reading with baby (oh yeah, that's why I'm doing this), mowing the lawn, exercise, field trips, filling out forms. If you're a Domestic Commando, you know what I'm talking about.

Each of these tasks is just one more spinning plate. And some days, all the plates come crashing down. And guilt blows into the house like some ill-mannered, fire-breathing dragon.

I have struggled with this issue for most of my career as a Domestic Commando. I felt I had to prove my value by exhausting myself—

preparing a multi-part to-do list each morning and dutifully marking off each accomplished task on the list by the end of the day.

Somehow, we have been misled to believe that we must be fully occupied with some task or another at all times or we are inadequate. This concept is not only foreign in most parts of the world, it is laughable.

The simple truth is that when we multitask, *nothing* receives our full attention. The task either takes longer to complete or it simply isn't accomplished to our satisfaction. Repeat after me:

> *When I multitask:*
> *Each task will take longer to do.*
> *Or*
> *The tasks may not be completed to the best of my ability.*

The end result is that something or, more importantly, someone (someone who deserves better, perhaps) is short-changed.

The art of efficiency does not come in multitasking or rushing. It comes in *prioritizing,* and Domestic Commandos must become proficient in prioritizing. This takes discipline.

Never list more than three high-priority items on your daily to-do list. One of those items should involve spending time with your kid(s): reading, playing, painting—something fun for both (or all) of you.

Beyond that, there are very few items, for me, that fall into the high-priority category. These include: paying bills, tax forms, doctor appointments, grocery shopping, laundry, and keeping the house clean. (Well, maybe not so much cleaning the house.)

Since you are only allowed two other big items per day, these have to be spread out over the course of the week or reformatted into smaller bites. For example, if you have a washer and dryer in your home, one or two loads can be done each day instead of having one designated wash day. On the other hand, having lived in apartments while growing up, I realize that going to a Laundromat requires a designated laundry day.

Similarly, you can do one big house cleaning per week, or you can break it up into smaller tasks to be done each day: vacuuming one day, mopping floors another day, cleaning bathrooms another, etc.

Find the battle plan that works for you, and make sure it reflects *your* priorities.

WISDOM SHARED

A Tale from the Trenches

Fresh eyes can be a great source of comfort and perspective.

One afternoon while waiting to pick up the kids at school, I was lamenting the fact that Second-born refused to wear the ankle socks that were part of her school uniform. She claimed the seam over the toes bothered her.

In desperation, I had bought her women's trouser socks, because the seam was at the end of the sock, so it shouldn't be so bothersome. Her response was to cut the tail ends of this seam so all her socks now had two holes, one on either side of the toes.

Oh, and did I mention that she also cut all the tags out of her shirts and blouses, leaving unseemly holes in her collars?

One of the moms present simply responded that, in the big picture, this really wasn't so bad. "Choose your battles," she wisely advised.

Those three words were a revelation! If I spent all my time micro-managing every single "imperfection" I would have depleted my energy and the credibility I'd need for the big, important battles (friends, curfews, anything influenced by peer pressure). The only smart strategy is to decide which battles are worth fighting and which ones really won't make a difference a month down the road.

I had been embarrassed that my daughter would be seen with these holes in her clothes and how it would reflect on me as her mother. But her clothes were always clean, and I tried diligently to remove the tags with a seam ripper before she could do the job herself.

Of course, just about the time she got over her tag aversion, manufacturers came out with tag-less shirts.

She still doesn't like socks.

CONNECTING

Hubby has always traveled a great deal for work. In fact, one year, he was out of town a total of 312 days.

While that year was an extreme example, it explains why a great deal of my approach to being a Domestic Commando involves self-reliance.

But exercising self-reliance doesn't mean that it's necessary or even good to be a lone commando. In the military, save the trained sniper, most of the elite commandos operate in teams. This has a lot of advantages in that there's always someone there to watch your back, and it provides a built-in social group of people who understand you, your training, and your mission.

Facebook and Twitter are nice diversions, but we need real connections. That's why it's important to step out and recruit. The easiest and most obvious place to start is with family. Although my immediate family lived out of state, I was lucky to have exceptional in-laws right in town. My mother-in-law and sister-in-law lived close by and provided welcome support and information.

There are other ways to connect, though, when you don't have the benefit of a ready-made support group. A house of worship is a good place to start if you are a person of faith.

You can look for a mom's morning-out program (generally offered by churches). These are usually offered once or twice a week from 9 a.m. to 1 p.m. The "problem" is that it's so tempting to schedule all the errands that are simply easier to accomplish without children in tow that it ceases to be mom's morning out and become mom's chore day. Instead, use this opportunity to meet a couple of the other moms and suggest an occasional get-together. It can be a light lunch (grown-ups only) or afternoon tea one day while the kids play nearby.

Or, you can schedule mom's night out. I was actually able to join a group of ladies once a month for dinner. The moms in this particular group were especially comfortable in their own skins. A couple of them were teachers who were now home-schooling their own kids. Another was a mother of four who had the brass to actually schedule a weekend for *herself* several times a year. She would check into a hotel *alone* and do whatever she chose to do while her husband fielded the kids for the weekend. She would read uninterrupted, take long baths and even polish her toenails without having to handle a crisis before the polish had dried completely. I learned a lot of wonderful attitude from being a part of the mom's night out gang.

Of course, it also was wonderful to go to a restaurant and have someone else serve *me* while I participated in a conversation! Even though I usually had to spend money on a sitter while most of the other moms had husbands in town to fill in for a couple of hours, I was delighted to be sharing a meal with other women with whom I had so much in common.

The monthly get-togethers lasted less than a year (it became impossible to schedule anything once summer rolled around), but it remains one of the best things I ever did for myself.

CIPHER

It comes as a devastating blow.

One day, you'll be dropping your child off at school or a friend's house and your customary "I love you" is met with a stern look and, perhaps, a whispered, "Mom! Not in front of everybody!"

As you swallow hard and make a mental note not to embarrass your child publicly again, it's important to realize that this does not mean that your child no longer needs you to express your love. The key is to do it discreetly.

In our family, codes provided the solution.

Before cell phones were everywhere and text messaging was even possible, my husband and I used to communicate by way of pagers. He could keep his pager on vibrate, and we could exchange messages using simple codes that didn't necessarily require a return call. For example,

143 meant "I love you."

A response of *1432* meant 'I love you, too.'

Of course, *911* meant there was an emergency with one of the children and would have elicited an immediate call.

So I introduced the concept of our own secret code with the kids. They enjoyed the idea and we came up with a system.

It was simple. I would squeeze their hand three times for "I love you." The response would be four squeezes back for "I love you, too." (Parents also need to hear this!) Or simply saying or texting "Three" almost always yields a "Four."

What's really great is the day that you child says, "Three," first.

SECURITY DETAIL

Anticipating consequences is the key to any good battle plan. When it comes to our family's safety, here are some of the tactics we've employed.

- We have never allowed our children to have any personalized clothing or backpacks. Their names have never been visible for a stranger to read their names and use it to his advantage by pretending he knows them.
- Whenever we traveled, I printed "business cards" for each child. These cards had my husband's name and mine, our home address, and our phone numbers, including cell phones. I would laminate several of these (or you can cover them with clear, adhesive shelf-liner). I would pin one to an inside pocket on whatever outfit each child was wearing that day. There was also a card in the water bottle holder that each child wore. They knew that these cards were for use in case they were ever separated from us.
- We have a code word or phrase that a child could use to secretly signal to me that she is not comfortable in a situation or something is not right. This could be an adjective that the child doesn't normally use, such as "nifty" or a phrase that sounds normal but is used out of context, such as, "I brought the blue shirt." As an example, I could call and ask how things are going. If I receive the coded response, I would grab my keys and head out the door. And my child was confident that Mama was on the way.
- The first time my children visited a new friend, I would drop him or her off myself so I could meet the parent(s), confirm that

there would be an adult present, and know how to return there quickly in case I received the emergency code.

- There should always be at least one standard, non-electric phone in the home. If you lose power, you can still make a call.
- I always keep a small flashlight in my purse. It's extremely handy in a poorly lit parking lot, in a stuck elevator or on a dark theme-park ride.

I CAN'T HELP BUT WONDER

- Why do toddlers always manage to slather their faces with petroleum jelly and/or mom's lipstick—and why can you never find the camera until the product has been smeared onto a number of non-washable surfaces? (Note: Getting the picture is what matters.)
- Why do babies and kids have more fun playing with the boxes the toys come in than with the toys themselves?
- Why do children's videos feature the most annoying songs and music?
- How come the first person in the pickup line at school is always the one whose child takes forever to get to the car?
- Why is it that the parent who can't attend the class party always sends in those expensive, store-bought cupcakes frosted with a three-inch glob of blue-tinted icing made with eight cups of sugar that stains everything it touches (your pants, your child's lips) and ensures that every single kid in class will be out of control?
- Why do extended warranties cover everything except what's wrong?
- Why do we use our "good" dishes only on holidays or when we have company?
- Why do clothing designers only care that their designs "hang right" so they display them on "human hangers"? Maybe they should learn to get past their two-dimensional designs and design clothes that hang right on healthy women.
- Why is it that the things that are supposed to improve our quality of life are so annoying? For example:
  - SUVs with their own zip codes, making the school pick-up line twice as long as it needs to be;

- Convenience foods that cause more guilt than they are convenient; (Ever read the ingredients lists? I took three years of college chemistry and can't pronounce a lot of that stuff.)
- Portable phones that always seem to need charging or have scratchy reception—assuming you can find the thing between the sofa cushions;
- Computers that get viruses and/or crash; (I live to back up my files.)
- The TV remote, which is perpetually MIA. (Is it mating with the portable phone underneath the sofa cushions? What horrible creature will that spawn?)

• Why do people with white dining room chairs always serve pasta with red sauce or a chocolate dessert when you have your kids with you?

And...

• Why is it that once you've dutifully draped the white chairs with a beach towel and laid your thick plastic mat (the one you keep in the car for such situations) under the chair, the meatball falls directly onto the floor, bounces once on the mat and *maliciously* rolls just onto the carpet?

EXIT STRATEGIES

I don't like surprises.

I usually prefer to know, in advance, how things will play out. When the kids were little, this wasn't a big problem.

Birthday parties and play dates usually came with a start and stop time. This could be placed on the schedule and you could work your daily routine around them.

But as the kids became older, I found I had to insist upon an exit strategy up front. If I didn't make them think about—and commit to—a time when sleepovers, LAN parties or "just hanging out" would end, I'd be on deck waiting to run a cab service or unable to accomplish the things that *I* needed to do.

So now there are no maneuvers approved without a predetermined exit strategy spelled out.

It's simply prudent.

YOU NEVER KNOW

I fully expected to be working full time when my kids entered high school.

Imagine my surprise when I found myself feeling conflicted once we finally reached this milestone.

I discovered that I liked being around the house so the kids could bring their friends over. I love the energy teenagers bring with them. I love seeing who my kids are hanging around with and being able to put faces to names. I love knowing they'll likely not get into too much trouble because they never know when I might pop my head into the room. Best of all, teens generally don't care if your house is spotless... I'm not sure they even notice.

My biggest challenge is the noticeable lack of junk food in my house. But you can never go wrong baking a batch of cookies when you have a couple of minutes (even if they are from a box mix).

MOVE IT, MOVE IT, MOVE IT!

There is no question that keeping up with children is exhausting. But the best remedy I have found for boosting my energy was inserting a 30-minute workout routine into my day. As Domestic Commandos, we work out to be healthy and strong, not to meet society's ludicrous standards of beauty. It helps us meet challenges both physical and mental while setting a positive example for our children.

The time devoted to regular activity should be non-negotiable (assuming your doctor has no objections). There are good, practical ways to fit a workout into your day.

I am not a gym person, so I have always preferred television exercise programs or videos. Thirty minute routines work well during nap times when babies are little, and can coincide with preschooler play times. In fact, your little one may even 'join' you, imitating some of your moves as you workout.

If you have a good, safe route within your neighborhood, you might opt for a *brisk* thirty minute walk. A regular stroller is fine for your child, no need to buy an expensive jogging stroller. Unless you live in a severely polluted city, the air outside is likely healthier than the recycled air inside your home. This is one of the big downsides to homes that are sealed airtight. Unless we air out our homes pretty frequently, we just concentrate the indoor chemicals, dust and fibers.

So get outside and get your babies outside. By making this a daily routine, you show respect for your body and your own well-being while introducing your children to the benefits of daily activity.

ASSETS

In the military, assets are to be protected from capture or destruction.

For a Domestic Commando, assets are the qualities that help us do our jobs every day. I've already addressed analysis and instinct. But probably the most important tool we have in our arsenal actually is a sense of humor.

Many of us are making the transition from the "working world," where we are expected to treat our work and assignments with steadfast seriousness. It's a humorless environment.

The job of raising decent human beings is as serious as it gets. But this is a *human* environment. Some days just aren't going to go well. In fact, some days are going to go really badly. But where is the joy if you take it out on your spouse, your kids, or yourself?

My early days as a Domestic Commando were unrelentingly serious. I can only imagine how much joy I might have missed. But it is *never* too late.

Train yourself to have a sense of humor. Take every opportunity you can to laugh and have fun. Rent funny movies. Read humorous books. Tell jokes with your kids. You should find reasons to laugh *every single day*.

These memories are the greatest gift you can give your family.

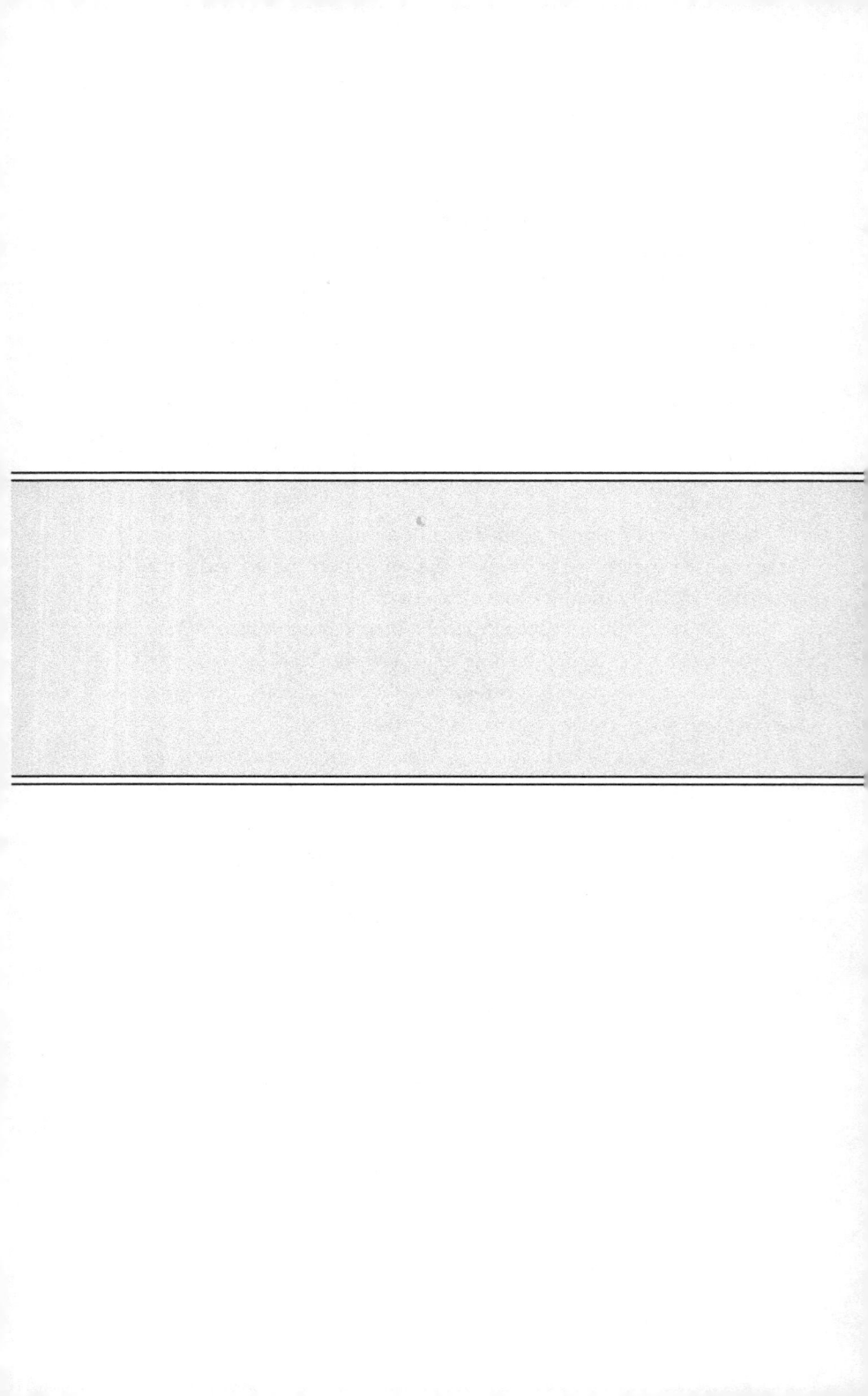

TACTICAL
OPERATIONS

Little Victories

REGARDING BABIES

- When your newborn is sleeping, you also should be sleeping.
- If breast feeding seems to be difficult, be patient. Give it at least two weeks before you give up. Every baby nurses differently, and it may take time for both of you to develop a "working" relationship. You owe it to yourself to experience the peaceful quiet of nursing, and you already know how good it is for your baby.
- Until you and your baby are comfortable nursing, it is best to nurse your baby in a room where only daddy is allowed to enter. This was the advice of our first pediatrician, a wonderful Cuban-born doctor who practiced in Northern Virginia. He explained that too much kibitzing from well-meaning moms and grandmothers can create frustration, which isn't good for nursing. Daddy simply isn't equipped to kibitz.
- Nursing is the best way to lose the baby weight without dieting. In fact, you need to keep up the healthy eating habits you adopted when you were pregnant as you really *are* eating for two people now.
- There's no need to take your baby out to crowded malls or events during the first few weeks of life. When you do venture out, carry your baby. Don't put baby in a stroller. That's where dust and germs are kicked up as people walk by—not to mention that strangers will actually reach in to touch your baby!
- Read to your baby every day, from the moment you bring him or her home. This will quickly become a welcomed part of the daily routine.
- Talk to your baby all the time. Describe what you're doing, whether it's washing dishes, mopping or going to the store. This is how your baby learns language.

- Play gentle tickle games with your baby as you recite nursery rhymes. There is a wonderful, hard-to-find book called *Baby Games* by Elaine Martin. Check online for a copy; it probably will be a used copy. It is all you need to play with your baby. I admit I needed to learn how to play.

VENUS AND MARS GO TO THE MALL

A Tale from the Trenches

It's something of a wonder that we survive our inexperience with our first child.

Somehow, even the simplest task is ridiculously complicated until we figure it out. By way of example, the first time my husband and I took our firstborn to a shopping mall was a study in extremes.

I carefully loaded the very attractive, dark blue diaper bag we had purchased at the baby store before he was even born. The bag had a changing pad that folded out of the side, multiple zippered compartments, and it was about the size of Montana. It took me the better part of an hour to pack it with what probably amounted to half a case of diapers and who-knows-how-many changes of clothes, plus receiving blankets, several burp cloths, wipes, multiple pacifiers (in case one fell and got dirty), and bottles (although I was nursing on demand). I believe there may have been a kitchen sink, if you dug all the way to the bottom.

The only thing bigger than the diaper bag was the baby carriage. Even in its folded, finger-squishing position, it rivaled the diaper bag in size. Oh, and I also had a kangaroo pouch to hold the baby in.

As my assembled necessities reached critical mass, I felt *nearly* ready to tackle what would likely amount to no more than a ninety-minute shopping trip.

My husband looked at this trunk-clogging collection of items and, in his most controlled voice, asked if we were going to be allowed to park in one of the handicapped spaces at the mall, because we clearly now had challenges we never had faced previously.

I ignored his comment, and off we went on what amounted to an uneventful excursion.

I eventually learned to pare down the list of items my child and I could not do without. The best diaper bag was, in fact, the smallest one I could find. A couple of diapers, a travel pack of wipes, a small bottle or juice box, a snack bag of cereal, an extra T-shirt, and a spare pacifier were good enough for most daily outings and errands.

Find the smallest bag that will hold these items, and you won't feel as though you are more pack mule than person.

FASHION STATEMENT

I called it "wearing my babies."

They actually lived on me for the first eighteen months of their lives. Each child started in the front carrier, or kangaroo pouch, for the first few months. This was a great way to get vacuuming done. Even a fussy baby often goes to sleep this way. Weird, but true.

When my back couldn't handle the weight of the front carrier any more, and my babies could sit up and support their heads, they went into a backpack. I could go anywhere and do almost anything with a kid in the backpack. Grocery shopping was a lot easier for me with Baby in the backpack. Of course, depth perception is crucial. You have to know just how close you can back up in an aisle to keep little hands from toppling the merchandise. But for the most part, the rider enjoyed looking over my shoulder to see what I was doing.

When Second-born came along, baby number one went into the stroller and the newcomer "wore Mama." Eventually, Firstborn wanted to be more mobile. That's when we met "Wrist Buddy" (aka the toddler leash. I preferred the sound of Wrist Buddy and had a much easier time introducing it this way).

I explained that the Wrist Buddy allowed Firstborn a little more freedom because he was too big for the backpack. But it was important to still be connected to Mama "so she wouldn't get lost and so bad people couldn't steal Firstborn."

I know that seems like an awful thing to say to a three-year-old, but I was very matter-of-fact with my kids that there are people who want to steal children. I said that it would make me very sad if that happened, and that the Wrist Buddy meant I could always see him. So the Wrist Buddy was our friend.

We practiced in the house with the Wrist Buddy. We practiced outside. It wasn't scary or uncomfortable. It was part of growing up. When we would arrive at the store or the mall, I would put Second-born into the backpack and help Firstborn out of the car seat. He would hold his hand out and say "Wrist Buddy." So, even if I was having a mommy-brain day, we never forgot to put it on.

TODDLERHOOD

Toddlers have a bad rap.

Parents are counseled by everyone to brace themselves for the terrible twos. If that is what you are expecting, that is what you'll get. I prefer to look at toddlers a little differently. It doesn't mean you won't be challenged, but toddlers really can be wonderful little people.

This stage is certainly different than babyhood because your toddler is no longer completely dependent on you for everything, especially mobility. He or she will be sampling independence and testing boundaries. Your patience and self-control will be on the front lines every day.

On the other hand, you can now read longer books to your little person. It's important to keep talking about everything you are doing or the things you are seeing for your child's language skills to continue to develop. Eventually, your child will begin to ask questions. Answer each of them to the best of your ability. The magical part will be when your child asks a question that inspires you to see the world through such fresh eyes. This is a gift from your child to you.

Think of your toddler as a little pal. He or she is no longer just accompanying you on errands, but can actively do things *with* you. This is a great time to play at the park, or go to the local children's museum or zoo. You can do things *together.* The key is to enjoy these outings in small doses because too much of even a good thing will wear a child down. All of a sudden, you may find yourself with a very whiny, exhausted child. Head straight for the car and go home for a nap.

But don't confuse exhaustion with the dreaded tantrum. Tantrums come complete with kicking, screaming, fist-pounding, and sometimes even side-to-side head shaking, as though she's saying, "No!" There is usually a trigger—an item the child wants but can't have, his desire to continue riding in the car rather than heading home, or some other unpredictable whimsy.

I learned to consider tantrums to be a temporary *short-circuit* in the child's wiring. This helped me deal with an episode in a completely detached manner. This is very important. While the first tantrum may be due to a short circuit, future tantrums are likely to be the result of being rewarded by receiving excessive attention or even the desired item.

Here is what worked for me:

Whether you are home or in a public place, do not say a word to your child. Pick him or her up and do a football carry across your hip to keep from being kicked too hard (if you are not home, go straight to the car. Wordlessly, and without making eye contact, put your child into the car seat. Obviously, this will be challenging, and you will likely be kicked or punched more than once. Do not react. Silently drive home.)

Put your child in the crib and close the door (this should be the safest place for your little one). Take the baby monitor, turned to low volume, to your room and lie down. Wait it out.

When the screaming stops, turn the monitor up. Your child will either be babbling and playing with a favorite toy, or sleeping, exhausted from the ordeal. Imagine how drained you would be if you had been that out of control.

Never discuss the incident with your child, or your heroic, detached behavior will be nullified.

The good news is that by behaving in a detached manner and not rewarding the tantrum, there will be very few, if any, repeats of the event. At least, that was my experience.

FLAK JACKET

Baby bibs are so cute. They have cute little pictures and sayings like, "I Love Grandpa," or "Daddy's Little Angel."

But they are functionally useless!

Let's be honest. By the time a child is starting to feed herself, the best a bib can do is provide a bib-shaped clean spot on the child's clothes.

I became painfully aware of this the first time I gave my kids spaghetti and meatballs. The floor was protected; the high chair could be hosed off; the kid could be dunked in the tub. But red sauce on clothes was another issue entirely.

I do not live to pre-treat.

That's when I came up with the spaghetti shirt.

Since we lived in an older home that we were constantly working on (painting, drywall mudding, tiling, etc.), I had appropriated a few of Hubby's older shirts that were big, comfortable, and "tired." I wore these to protect my clothes.

I applied the same principle to the kids. In my dresser, I had T-shirts that had seen better days. Because they were smaller than my husband's shirts, they were a better fit, but were still big enough to easily slip over a fully dressed child. These were enlisted as spaghetti shirts.

Spaghetti shirts were used any time there was something particularly messy to be eaten, or whenever we pulled out brushes and paint for artistic expression.

One name, but an all-purpose shirt.

GREAT EXPECTATIONS

Have you had this experience yet? An older member of the family or an elderly friend watches your diaper-clad toddler running by in the pursuit of some joyful activity. The observer comments that *her* children were all potty-trained by twelve to eighteen months. You can hear the disapproval in the unspoken question: Why is your toddler still in diapers?

Despite reading again and again that potty training isn't going to be successful until a child is two and a half to three years old, I kept hearing the same comments from the older generation. Yet, I didn't know too many moms in my age group who had successfully potty trained early. I began to think there had to be a reason for this difference.

Then one day, the old light bulb came on. Why in the world would our kids *want* to become potty-trained? They were clad in these amazing disposable diapers designed to keep them as comfortable as possible! Hello? Where's the motivation in that?

So, faced with a six-month-old and a three-year-old who was totally content with the disposable-diaper status quo, I decided to try an experiment. Armed with some quality diaper covers (they look like disposable diapers, but they have Velcro attachments and are washable) and a diaper service, my oldest went into cloth diapers.

Since the weekly cost for the diaper service was comparable to the cost of disposables, it was not a financially risky experiment.

Suddenly, it was no longer very comfy or convenient to be wearing a diaper. In fact, it was downright yucky!

Potty training took just six weeks, bolstered by reminders that using the potty resulted in greater comfort.

Other friends tried this system with similar results. However, we all waited until the kids were at least two and a half before attempting potty training.

GOODBYE PACIFIER DAY

Yes, I gave my babies pacifiers.

It was a completely calculated move on my part.

I had once seen a child of nine or ten pitifully sucking her thumb as she waited in the pediatrician's office. I realized that if my children sucked their thumbs, it was going to be a very difficult habit to break. Thumbs are just so available.

So I figured a pacifier would be preferable. When the time came, you could take a pacifier away, unlike those ubiquitous thumbs.

As it turned out, my kids really enjoyed their pacifiers. And the pacifier "carcasses" were everywhere: under the table, behind a chair, between the cushions on the couch. It was like squirrels came in and stored pacifiers instead of nuts.

Of course, the pacifiers were nowhere to be found when we desperately needed one. Yet, I can't tell you how many times I would suddenly see a child with a pacifier where there hadn't been one just a moment earlier. His first magic trick!

Frankly, I let my kids have their pacifiers long after the experts said they should no longer have them. But, I let them have them *just long enough*.

When Firstborn turned two, he began attending "Wilma's Little People's School" for two hours, twice a week. Because there weren't any children in our neighborhood, I signed him up so that he could be around other little kids every now and then. The first day of "school," I suggested he leave his pacifier behind as I unhooked the straps of his car seat. "Pop!" Out came the pacifier. He placed it in the car seat, and it was there when he returned. Every day he attended, we would repeat the scenario, and he would leave the pacifier behind. I was pleased that he could manage without it during "class."

This continued for several months, until Firstborn got a bad cold. I decided, rightly or wrongly, that it had to be caused by germs from less-than-pristine pacifiers. So, I created "Goodbye Pacifier Day." I marked it for Friday, one week away. I explained that it was time for pacifiers to go away; I showed him where "today" was on the calendar; and then counted to Goodbye Pacifier Day, a week later on a Friday.

Frankly, two-year-olds don't have much of a concept of time. I knew that. So every morning, I would show him the calendar. And then I'd count how many daytimes and nighttimes there would be until Goodbye Pacifier Day.

We had already collected all of the errant pacifiers in the house and made them disappear. We went to the store, and Firstborn selected his last pacifier. This was the only pacifier in the house for that final week.

On the morning of Goodbye Pacifier Day, I pointed to the calendar and reminded him that this was the day. Then I ignored the pacifier for the rest of the morning. He used it at will. Finally, lunchtime arrived.

The pacifier was discarded for lunchtime favorites. While Firstborn was occupied with the meal, Mama painted the business end of the pacifier with the liquid sold to stop nail biting, and returned it to its spot.

After lunch, "Pop!" In goes the pacifier. Mama acts disinterested nearby. A couple of drags, and out pops the pacifier.

Firstborn scrunches up his face. "The pacifier tastes juicy!" Unlike most children, this was not a favorable comment, since this child didn't like juice.

"Oh!" replies Mama. "Oh, my gosh! It's Goodbye Pacifier Day. I forgot! But the pacifier remembered and got juicy to remind you. Yucky pacifier. I guess we don't want it anymore."

"No!"

Over the next couple of days, I had to remind him—mostly before bedtime—that the pacifier still tasted yucky. But he was a trouper who was ready to be over the pacifier and just needed a little ceremony to help make the transition.

Two and a half years later, the scenario replayed itself with Secondborn. She, too, would leave her pacifier behind when she went to class, which was my signal that she would be ready for Goodbye Pacifier Day in a few months.

The "last pacifiers" are stored in our family's Heirloom Box (see Ready Packs) as mementos of our children's first rite of passage.

TRADITIONS

One of the best parts of being a Domestic Commando is that we have the time and energy to focus on family traditions.

There is tremendous comfort in things familiar.

You can begin by honoring the traditions you and your spouse grew up with: special recipes, birthday songs, holiday decorations—whatever triggers happy memories.

Most of our traditions revolve around food (surprise!). Thanksgiving in our house is served up Southern style, as that was my family's tradition. This means simple but delicious cornbread dressing and sweet potatoes. I no longer bake the sweet potatoes with marshmallows, but they are still a key side dish.

Christmas meals worked out especially well, since my family served a traditional Cuban meal on Christmas Eve and Hubby's family served its special meal on Christmas Day. Every Christmas Eve, I prepare black beans and rice with roast pork. Christmas Day, we would go to my mother-in-law's home for the Carpenters' traditional meal, which included a whole, baked beef tenderloin, mashed potatoes, and Aunt Ruth's Steak Sauce. When my mother-in-law passed away, I continued the tradition, and everyone helps make the side dishes.

Of course, not all traditions revolve around food, and some traditions just happen.

When Hubby and I were first married, my father and step-mother would send us a dated ornament for the tree every year. When the children were born, we bought each of them an ornament for the year of their birth. Every year, after the strands of lights are strung onto the tree and the angel topper is in place, the first ornament placed on the tree is the one from the year we were married, the year our household was established. The commemorative ornaments are then hung in order, with the kids placing their own ornament on the tree. Next, we hang the ornaments that have been made by the kids. Everything else just fills in the blanks around these treasures. Our tree is not glamorous or trendy. But it is beautiful and meaningful to our family.

Whether we are setting out empty Easter baskets to be filled overnight, or using the pewter candle holders my mother-in-law gave us for birthday cakes and pies, or making our first toast of "Here's to the absent ones" at holiday meals, I am unabashedly militant about protecting and preserving our family traditions.

HOLIDAY S.O.P.

One of the most frustrating transitions I faced when I became a Domestic Commando had to do with special occasions, especially holiday dinners.

I was raised to be on time—always! Therefore, we were almost always out the door and on our way at the necessary time.

The problem was that, for some reason, getting the kids ready always filled the amount of time available, no matter how far ahead I started preparations. Consequently, I didn't make it into the shower with enough time to get dressed, let alone dry my hair and put on makeup.

After poking myself in the eye for the umpteenth time with a mascara wand as Hubby drove us to his mom's house, I vowed to come up with a better system. It had to be possible!

The answer was embarrassingly simple: I got ready first!

I took my shower before everyone else. Then the kids got their baths while my hair started to dry. After they were dressed in their good clothes, I put on their spaghetti shirts so they could snack and play without messing up their outfits. I put on one of Hubby's old button-front dress shirts to protect my outfit. It was loose enough not to wrinkle my clothes, and was my own version of a spaghetti shirt. Next, I did my hair and makeup. Last step: spaghetti shirts off and everyone out the door.

With this simple change in procedure, I left the house looking my best and was able to relax and enjoy the day.

UN-WRAPPED

Our first Christmas as parents was a revelation about how every family has their own way of doing things.

My husband fully expected to wrap all of those oversized boxes from Santa. (You know, the size of the box is inversely proportional to the size of the child. That is, the smaller the child, the bigger the box.)

Now, in my childhood home, Santa just left everything out in the open on Christmas Eve for discovery the next morning. Only gifts from family were wrapped.

I tried to explain to my husband that Santa didn't have the time, patience, or desire to kill that many trees in order to wrap these enormous boxes. Nonetheless, the gifts arrived all wrapped up. I thought it a terrible waste.

The answer to our dilemma came a couple years later when we were faced with Santa gifts for two children. And the answer was right next door.

I was visiting our neighbor, Phyllis, when I noticed large, misshapen fabric bags in front of her tree. Each bag had its own colors and patterns and was individually tagged with the name of a family member.

This was how they exchanged gifts: They just dropped each present in the appropriate bag to be "unwrapped" Christmas morning.

I loved the idea! I just had to modify it for our family to achieve some sort of compromise.

I bought several yards of red flannel and some cording. I made two identical Santa Bags, one for each child. We wrapped the gifts that went under the tree for family and friends. But on Christmas morning, Santa would leave the gifts for each child in his or her own big, red bag.

No more wrapping into the wee hours of the morning, and no more wasted wrapping paper (we're talking less than six hours of use, in some cases). Instead, we have a practical, time-saving, picture-perfect tradition that we all look forward to every Christmas morning.

BASKET REMIX

I took much the same approach with Easter Baskets as I did with the Santa Bags.

I didn't buy new baskets every year; instead, every family member had their own basket which we stored and re-used. Saturday night, the kids would set out their empty baskets in the family room, awaiting the Easter Bunny's visit. In the morning, the baskets would be filled with toys, books, videos, and some candy.

I really enjoyed finding fun things to put in the baskets. The kids' baskets were never like anyone else's, and I liked having control over exactly what went into them.

This was so much fun for me that I extended the tradition to the adults in my life, as well. Before my mother-in-law passed away, I would look for goodies for her when I shopped for the kids' baskets. She enjoyed the funny little things I put in the basket as much as I enjoyed collecting them.

SHIFT CHANGE

A Tale from the Trenches

I'm not sure anyone else has ever experienced this phenomenon, but I have to bring it up. It concerns my kids and how they behave.

My children were born two and a half years apart. They engaged in the usual sibling animosity and had totally different agendas. Yet they were completely coordinated in one thing: They took turns being wretched.

For some reason, I've been lucky that the kids didn't go through any challenging phase at the same time. Generally, I've been exasperated with the actions (or inactions) of only one child at a time (of course, this didn't include the frequent sibling battles; I ignored those as much as possible).

I'm not certain if this miracle is an act of God, a manifestation of a cycle of nature, luck, or simply a coordinated conspiracy.

If it's the latter, I'd just like to know where my kids were keeping their time cards for the next shift change.

CLASS WORK

One of the advantages of being full-time Domestic Commandos is that we're available to help out at the children's school.

Field trips and class parties are the main opportunities to volunteer, and our elementary school generally had the schedule for the year prepared in advance. Sign-up sheets were set out at the first open house.

There was always one mom in every class who signed up for *everything*. The problem with this kind of generosity is that it sometimes doesn't leave much room for others to participate.

I learned to wait to fill out the sign-up sheets. That way, parents who worked outside the home and had fewer opportunities to participate had a better chance to find a spot they could fill.

Even though my schedule was comparatively more flexible, I would still come to Open House armed with my personal calendar so that I didn't double-book a day. This is especially important when you have more than one child in school and are scheduling for multiple classes.

It was also helpful that I didn't have any preference about which party or field trip(s) I helped with. Since it was all about the kids, I preferred to fill in where there wasn't as much interest.

As far as party food was concerned, I wish I could say that there was something fabulous and special that I made. But the truth is I became known as the mom who sent in the cheese platters.

I didn't even realize this was the case until my firstborn was in fifth grade, and I was preparing a platter for one of the holiday parties. I had a variety of fruit on the counter, and he asked me what I was doing. When I explained, he said, "No. You have always made cheese platters, and I have always taken cheese platters. That's what everyone expects me to bring, and it's the only thing I like to eat."

Stunned by this revelation and concerned that my child should have something to eat at his holiday party, I proceeded to pull blocks of cheese out of the refrigerator. I cubed them into wavy, bite-size pieces with a crinkle-cutter blade, as I had countless times before. I then finished the fruit tray and sent that, as well, since that's what I had signed up for.

When it came to field trips, I'm sure I was considered the loner parent. Most often, the other parent-volunteers could be found at the front of the group with the teacher, or a splinter group would be about halfway back, talking enthusiastically about one thing or another.

Generally, I could be found at the back of the line of children, taking head counts. I felt my mission was to make sure no one's baby went missing. Since I'm not very good at small talk, this self-imposed assignment suited me well.

ONE OF THESE KIDS IS NOT LIKE THE OTHER

A Tale from the Trenches

My children are polar opposites.

They have different interests, different personalities, different priorities, different everything! Yet they have the same parents and have grown up in the same house.

One likes boats; the other does not. One lives for computer games; the other prefers to text message friends. One likes virtually every kind of music, played as loudly as possible; the other finds a smaller range of music acceptable and only when played at low volume. One is an old soul; the other has the heart of an adventurer.

The challenge (other than the constant fighting) has been to enable and encourage each child individually. This means acknowledging and accepting their individual traits and not making comparisons.

But just as challenging has been the need to cope with how each child views and deals with the world beyond our front door. One year, one of our children refused to participate in the fifth-grade graduation program. I was called in. I quickly became aware that, in addition to the ceremony, there was a musically oriented segment, with the students playing recorders and singing. This is something my child has never been comfortable with.

The shock was unmistakable when I said I was fine with my child's decision, and I would not force him to take part in the performance. He did not have a crucial role. No one was counting on his participation.

After attending the maudlin production, I told my child that I agreed with his choice not to participate.

It was not the politically correct answer; but for him, it was absolutely the right decision.

TEACHER APPRECIATION

My children attended a wonderful, small elementary school that fostered some very interesting perspectives. Not only did the principal encourage class participation from as many parents as possible so that no single parent monopolized the classroom, but she also expressed her opinion that children should make, rather than purchase, gifts for their teachers. In effect, it made the playing field level for all of the children, and also made the gift more thoughtful. By creating the gift, the child actually gave something of herself, as opposed to something Mom or Dad just picked up at a store.

I personally like giving and receiving small food gifts because the recipient doesn't have to worry about where to store another clever little trinket. After a few years, where could a teacher possibly keep all those "I ♥ Teacher" ceramic apples?

For our part, we began the tradition of making and giving homemade chocolate truffles.

Truffles worked out perfectly for our family. These rich little morsels were tasty and easy to make. It made for a fun, low-stress event that my children looked forward to each year.

Truffle "Dough"
- 1 pound semi-sweet chocolate chips (you will need two bags to get 16 ounces)
- 1 cup heavy whipping cream

Truffle Decorations
- coconut
- chopped walnuts
- coco powder
- jimmies or sprinkles (decorative, edible toppings found in the cake-decorating department)

Bring cream to a simmer over medium heat in a heavy-bottom sauce pot. Reduce heat to low and add chocolate, stirring until smooth. Transfer mixture to a bowl and refrigerate until it firms up, about two hours.

It is now "hand-washing time." Once a year, I knew my kids' hands were absolutely sanitary because they would wash them an extra long time and scrub them with a nail brush before making the truffles.

Next, we line up some bowls for the decorating phase. Low, rimmed soup bowls work well because little hands can get in and roll the truffle around without too much trouble.

Armed with a teaspoon, each child scoops up some truffle dough and rolls it into a ball. Then, he drops the truffle into one of the bowls of decorations and rolls it around to coat it. Cool, dry hands make it easier to form the truffles, so we stop a couple of times to rinse off chocolaty palms.

The kids then place each finished truffle into a tiny paper cup. You can find these in some grocery stores or in craft shops that have cake- and candy-making departments. They look like tiny muffin liners.

We assemble a variety-pack of truffles, loading them into little metal gift tins from a dollar discount store, or small boxes that the children decorate. Armed with a bag of homemade goodies, each child delivers the gifts to resource teachers, the school secretary, and the principal, as well as the primary teacher.

Older children can prepare chocolate-dipped pretzels (use the big, fat pretzel sticks) or homemade cookies. These can be packaged in the cellophane bags that florists use for corsages or wrapped in colored plastic wrap and placed in a gift bag, basket or mug.

If you prefer non-food gifts items, consider the following:
- a note pad imprinted with the teacher's name;
- a student-decorated picture frame with a picture from a class party or field trip;
- gift cards (from an office supply, video, craft, or book store) presented with flowers and a handmade card;
- a hardy indoor plant.

LAMAZE CLASS, RECYCLED

The idea of natural childbirth has been romanticized in the past half century as though it were some brilliant, Nobel Prize-worthy discovery.

Of course, with the exception of the last hundred years or so, women have been giving birth without drugs for millennia. On the other hand, as my husband points out, we put a man on the moon in 1969, so why should childbirth have to be painful?

Since the idea of not being conscious and aware at such an extraordinary moment is hardly appealing, we dutifully attended our Lamaze classes and learned to breathe and pant with the best of them.

I must confess, however, that no number of cleansing breaths could put a dent in a Pitocin-fueled contraction. To this day, the only words I remember speaking to my husband were, "Find somebody with drugs." Likewise, the only medical person I can still name was the anesthesiologist who performed the epidural.

However, my Lamaze classes did not go to waste. Fifteen years later, I once again turned to the calming effects of those techniques as I sat in the co-pilot's seat of the family car, enduring yet another painful rite of passage: a teenager with a learner's permit.

It goes something like this:
- employ quick pants as catastrophe looms;
- grab the door handle until knuckles turn white;
- crisis passes;
- take a deep, cleansing breath;
- slowly release the door handle, allowing blood to return to the fingers;
- employ quick pants as disaster, again, is imminent;
- jam right foot onto imaginary brake pedal;
- try to ignore disgruntled sounds coming from driver;

- take a deep, cleansing breath;
- repeat as needed;
- give thanks when it's all over;
- hug your baby.

INSIGHT

A Tale from the Trenches

Teenagers are a species unto themselves. They sleep...a lot. They should be required to experience sunlight in order to keep them free of mildew.

The following is the text of a note I wrote in the car and sent in to my son's first-period teacher one morning:

Dear Mr. _____:

I am sorry for my son's late arrival, but like the sap of a tree in winter, he just doesn't move unless you light a fire under him. I was out of matches.

(signed) Toni Carpenter

FACE TIME

When they are not sleeping, teenagers are very busy people.

The problem is they are always busy doing things which, in their opinion, should not include old persons (like their parents).

Frankly, this is a natural progression. After all, it's your job to raise independent, productive people. But that doesn't mean that all contact should cease. There are still values to reinforce and information to pass along. The problem is getting on the schedule, so it's a matter of taking and making the opportunities for face time.

My favorite technique is to schedule a date, one on one. A casual, "Let's go to lunch," is usually well received and doesn't interfere too much with other social obligations (not to mention, food is involved).

The public nature of going out means the conversation is casual and, preferably, non-controversial. Just be together.

STREAMLINING

I'm rather bewildered when I see women lugging enormous handbags as they go about their day.

What in the world do they have in there, and is the back pain really worth the convenience of having it along for the ride?

It may be a reaction to my pack-mule experience as a new mother, but I seek out the smallest purse that will accommodate my must-have items. (See Purse Pack.)

I clip my sunglasses case to the outside of my bag. If there is a little extra room inside, I'll add trial-size tubes of hand lotion and anti-bacterial gel.

Believe it or not, you really don't need more than this on most days. It's one thing to be toting a child on your hip; it's another matter entirely to be hauling inanimate objects around just in case you might need them.

KEYS TO SAFETY

It's important to be aware of your surroundings when out and about, but it's also important to plan for possible problems.

One evening as I was headed into a discount store, I saw a woman walking through the busy parking lot holding a child by the hand. Suddenly, a man came by at a full run and grabbed her purse, knocking the woman *and* the child to the ground. As several people ran to help her (she was shaken but okay), others took off after the thief.

This experience reminded me how important it is to always be on guard, especially when my children are with me. Furthermore, it taught me never to carry my car keys or my cell phone in my purse.

I keep my keys on a clip called a carabiner. These can be bought almost everywhere and are inexpensive. I use it to clip my keys to my belt loop, which keeps my hands free. If ever a creep tries to grab my purse, he won't have my house keys *and* my address. Just as important, I won't be stranded somewhere without transportation.

Whenever possible, keep your cell phone in your pocket, or on a belt clip.

THE HOME FRONT

Clutter is the Enemy: This is the first rule of housekeeping engagement.

For every little knick-knack you have on display, for every stack of newspapers, magazines, and catalogs that you have piled up, you've detracted from how tidy your home is and added to the amount of dusting you have to do.

If you've collected a lot of "stuff," try giving at least half of it a rest in a closet or cupboard. Your home will immediately seem bigger and more airy. And you'll actually be able to appreciate the things you've left on display because they won't be competing for attention. Then, when you're ready for a change, rather than spend a bunch of money on *more* stuff, bring out some of the stored reinforcements to give the display pieces a rest.

To minimize the paper clutter, recycle newspapers and magazines as soon as possible. Better still, use online sources to eliminate the paper altogether. Also, try keeping a big basket by the chair in your family room for catalogs and magazines you're not quite ready to recycle. This keeps the stacks off the tables and keeps things looking tidy.

Mastering the Mail: Set up a designated space to deal with the mail. I take it to the laundry room, which is adjacent to my kitchen, where there is a letter opener, a basket for paper to be recycled, a trash can, and a paper shredder. "Real" mail (bills, cards, bank statements) is set aside. Unwanted catalogs go straight into the recycle basket. Junk mail is opened and all credit card offers are shredded. Empty envelopes go into the trash can.

The Eight O'clock Rule: When my kids were little and went to bed relatively early, I established this rule for my own benefit. I would make certain that I tidied up the main rooms of the house *before* eight o'clock, so that I could enjoy some downtime without a mess prodding me into housekeeping rather than relaxing. Since the children were in bed, the place was going to stay tidy, which meant I also woke up to a fresh start in the morning.

Joy of Carpet Sweeping: I hate vacuuming. I hate the clunky equipment, I hate moving from outlet to outlet, I hate the noise, and I hate the hassle. I don't even like carpeting—just because it needs to be vacuumed. I do however, like the way the carpet looks when it has been vacuumed. But there is no way I will ever be one of those people who vacuums every day. So for quick work, I have found there is nothing better than an old-fashioned carpet sweeper. They are cheap, they don't need to be plugged in, they weigh almost nothing, they're easy to empty and they'll get noticeable stuff like leaves and bits of paper off the carpet in almost no time.

THE AMBUSH

Special occasions and holidays are a great excuse to fluff up the house and prepare favorite recipes for family and friends.

Unfortunately, some visits are unplanned and, often, inconvenient. Maybe it was an "ouchy day" for your child or for you. Maybe you've just spent a week nursing a couple of kids with chicken pox. Whatever the reason, your home probably does not look its best. After being caught off-guard too many times, I developed a couple of battle plans for unexpected guests.

Plan 1 (half-hour notice)
- Wipe off the kitchen counters and clean the sink.
- Clean the toilet (leave the blue stuff in), and close the shower curtain.
- Pick up the obvious stuff with the carpet sweeper.
- Move the cat off the dining room table and polish the table.
- Move the cat off the coffee table, put it in your room, and close the door. (Polish the coffee table last so it still smells good when guests arrive.)
- Put on a clean outfit, or at least change your shirt.
- Brush your hair, and put on lipstick and blush.

Plan 2 (unexpected guests already at the door)
- Smooth down your hair and open the door holding the vacuum cleaner or broom that you keep near the front door for just such an occasion. (They'll believe they've interrupted your efforts and will hopefully feel lousy for showing up unexpectedly. With any luck, they will leave.)

TO RIDE AND ROLL

A Tale from the Trenches

Our home sits on a large lot. Not by choice, it just happened that way.

My hubby, being a guy, was delighted when he had no choice but to buy a riding lawn mower. Frankly, the grass grows so fast in the summer that by the time you finished with a push mower, you'd have to start mowing all over again.

Then, there's the "hundreds factor." In the summer, it can get up to one hundred degrees with one hundred percent humidity. There is serious question as to whether one can survive that amount of mowing under those conditions. So we became the proud owners of a riding lawn mower that my husband truly seemed to enjoy operating. The problem was his work frequently took him out of town for weeks at a time.

The grass, however, was not mindful of his schedule, and inconveniently continued to grow at a remarkable pace. And I became conflicted.

Quite simply, the "chick" in me did not want to operate the manly lawn tractor. It was a big machine that made a lot of noise, kicked up all manner of dust and dirt, and our climate made it very sweaty work, indeed.

But the Domestic Commando in me couldn't stand to look at the tall grass knowing that a tidy lawn was just a mower session away. So I took action.

I called my husband and asked him how to run the beast. He gave me the procedures and reminded me to only mow up and down where the yard slopes because if I mowed side to side, the machine might roll over on me (*not* what I wanted to hear).

I cleverly hired a babysitter, so my kids wouldn't starve to death in case the lawn tractor rolled over on me and my body wasn't found for weeks. (Okay, I'm a little paranoid.)

I put on some grubby clothes, sat on the mower, pushed the choke lever all the way up to the rabbit symbol at the top, depressed the brake, and turned the key.

R-r-r-r, the engine cranked. Then it caught. *Whir*, it whined. I slid the choke lever down to the turtle symbol... harrumph! It stalled out. *Okay, let's try that again.*

This time, I slid the choke lever halfway between the rabbit and the turtle. *Budden, budden, budden,* it rumbled.

Okay, time to engage the blades. I rotated the big lever through its arc. *Whee,* the blades screamed. (*Stay cool,* I said to myself. *You* are *a Domestic Commando.*)

I slid the speed lever from neutral to the third slot, released the clutch and...*I'm mowing!*

Hoo ya! I am controlling this machine and making it do what I need it to do. It's mowing my overgrown lawn! What a hoot!

An hour and a half later, I climbed off, my lawn mowed.

I was tired, sweaty and just plain gross. I was also victorious.

I have learned several important things from mowing the lawn:
- Follow all the safety rules that come with the mower.
- Never mow between 10 a.m. and 2 p.m. Just as you should avoid the sun during those times when sunbathing, it's going to be awfully intense even on a lawn tractor.
- You can't hear the phone ring when you're mowing. (I love this part!)
- Always wear protective clothing when mowing. Despite the heat, I like to wear long pants, a big T-shirt, work boots and gloves (to keep my hands from slipping on the wheel—it doesn't come with power steering).
- If the idea of operating a mower terrifies you, DON'T DO IT.

ANALOG MEMORIES

I have always been amazed by people who can spout off the date or year of an important or noteworthy event (e.g. the blizzard of '85 or whatever).

I have not been gifted with such a memory.

This is why the family calendar that hangs in our kitchen is so important.

When I select the new calendar each December (it's always a gift to the family from Santa), I know it's not merely decoration. It's a document of our lives.

I use it to mark vacations; the passing of family members, including pets; natural and manmade disasters; and special, unexpected occasions.

At the end of the year, I use it to transfer birthdays and anniversaries to the next year's calendar. The old calendar is saved in our family Heirloom Box as a memento of the year gone by.

NOT-SO-CRAFTY

I was not born with the crafting gene.

In fact, you might say that I am among the craft-challenged. Here's the proof:

- I own a glue gun. My husband has used it more than I have.
- I look at a silk flower arrangement and think, *Dust*.
- I do not own a bottle of shellac, nor do I *want* to own a bottle of shellac.

And that's okay.

I have found other ways to channel creative energy.

- I tore out a bathroom when I was five months pregnant, and was tiling the tub surround at seven months pregnant.
- I have laid flooring.
- I have taped and mudded drywall (not really all that well, but the price was right).
- I have wallpapered bathrooms and children's rooms (too well, I discovered when it came time to remove the wallpaper. Decorative paint techniques are much easier to "remove." Just slap on another coat of paint!)
- I enjoy cooking and find tremendous satisfaction in preparing and presenting a creamy risotto or a hearty pot roast.
- I've learned to design little centerpieces that fulfill my own personal aesthetic but don't require crafting skills.

Everyone should be encouraged to develop her own personal style, based upon what she enjoys doing and what she is good at. I'm sure there are lots of Domestic Commandos with excellent crafting skills.

I'm just not one of them.

POWER PLAY

My husband has more tools than a neighborhood hardware store. I think he has every type of tool possible. I think he's actually used everything he has, but I'm not sure.

It's a guy thing, I guess.

On the other hand, I've found it's quite helpful to have some tools of my own. I keep them in a cupboard that he never looks in. This way, they are always ready when I need them. He also can't accuse me of using his tools and not putting them back where they belong—because I didn't use them in the first place!

I have my own power drill; I had a cordless, rechargeable drill for awhile but I didn't like it. The batteries made the drill heavier, and it always seemed to need recharging at an inconvenient time. So now I have a corded drill, and I keep a heavy-duty extension cord handy to let me reach most anywhere. I also prefer a drill that doesn't require a chuck key to lock the bits in place. If the chuck key gets lost, the drill becomes useless to me.

Using a power drill is simply wonderful. Once you've assembled a do-it-yourself organizer, shelving unit, or cabinet, or installed child-safety latches with a power drill, you'll never go back to a manual screwdriver.

I also bought my own set of bits and screw heads.

Of course, it's still helpful to have a basic set of screwdrivers for those things you can't use a power drill on, like bicycles and cabinet hinges.

For the shear rush of efficiently and easily accomplishing an otherwise daunting task, the power drill ranks right up there with the lawn tractor.

Roger that!

Tactical Op: If you need to replace or repair a part, take the old part with you to the home improvement store. Hand it to an employee in the appropriate department and say, "I need one of these." You'll save time and money because you won't buy the wrong item, and you won't have to make several return trips.

A SCIENTIFIC MYSTERY

A Tale from the Trenches

Despite many years of science education, I believe the only people who do not believe in spontaneous generation have never done laundry.

No matter how many loads I've done in a day, I have never seen the bottom of three empty hampers at the same time. My husband and I share a hamper, and the kids have their own hampers in their rooms.

Actually, I don't know why they have hampers.

My kids do not use their hampers until they realize they do not have any clean clothes (unfortunately, spontaneously generating clothing does not come in the clean variety...only dirty). Then they pile the hampers to overflowing, drag them to the laundry room during the night, and wonder why I don't have clean clothes for them the next morning as they are getting ready for school.

"By the way, what am I supposed to do with your clothes when they're clean?"

"I brought you hangers!"

"No, you didn't."

"How would you know? You don't know everything!"

"Yes, I do."

After all these years, you'd think they would realize that I have given everyone in the family a different colored set of hangers, so I can tell who really did bring hangers, and who just says she did.

MAMA'S LOGS

They are undeniably the most accommodating organizational tool you can buy, and they are downright inexpensive!

Three-ring binders are simply wonderful things. I use them to organize and compile things that are too unwieldy for a standard file folder.

- I keep one binder to log car maintenance and repairs. Most of the invoices are on standard 8½-by-11 sheets. Just punch the three holes in the invoice and pop it into the binder. You can organize it any way you want. I keep a divider for each vehicle and store the most recent pages right on top.
- I use a similar system for home maintenance and repair. This is divided up by home systems: air conditioning, plumbing, roofing, etc. New dividers can be added as needed. This system keeps a running record of all the work you've had done. After a while, it's hard for me to remember each service performed and who performed it.
- This is also the perfect place to keep information on service contracts, such as annual inspections and air conditioner maintenance.
- I've also come to use a three-ring binder for favorite recipes. The pages are nice and big, it's easy to update, and most Internet recipes print out as a standard-sized page. Divide the binder up any way you like to make it easy for you to find what you need. Choose a binder that has pockets inside as a place to temporarily store recipes you've clipped. When you have a chance, type them up, punch the holes, and add them to your recipe collection. Or keep some plastic page protectors right in the binder and slip clipped recipes into these sleeves.

- Perhaps one of the most helpful uses I've found for three-ring binders is keeping track of school handouts. In an effort to keep parents informed, schools often pass along myriad pages of notices, from calendars to events to fund-raisers. I keep a binder for each child, storing the parent handbooks and student directories in the binder pockets. I keep the binders and a three-hole punch handy on a bookshelf near the kitchen. I can't begin to imagine the time I've saved because I don't have to hunt for loose papers all the time. At the end of the year, most papers can go into the recycle bin, and the binder is ready for the next school year.

RANK AND FILE

I live by business cards. I am always collecting the cards of contractors, repair companies, service providers, etc. I use them to make my own version of a Domestic Commando Better Business Roster.

I had to come up with this system because I have a terrible memory for names, whether it's a person's name or a company's name. Just as important, there is a huge difference in the quality, fairness, and even honesty of different service providers. So this is my simple way of keeping track of the good guys and the bad guys.

The only thing you need is an old-fashioned business card file that you can keep in a convenient spot. You'll divide it into three sections: Call First, New Contacts, and Never Again.

Each time you have some kind of service, repair, or installation done, ask for a card. After the contractor leaves, make appropriate notes on the card and put it in your card file under Call First or Never Again. Did she clean up after herself or leave you a mess? Was he on time? Did she honor her estimate? Did he dawdle for an hour and a half, then poke his head around for a few minutes, say he couldn't find a problem and charge you for a two-hour visit? Did he give you the creeps? Your impressions and opinion are the only things that count.

Next time you need to hire someone, go to the Call First section and make your choice from a card in that section. If you don't have a card for the service needed, check to see if you have any cards in the New Contact section that fit the bill. This is the spot you'll use to save cards you collected for future reference.

If New Contacts has nothing to offer, the phone book or the internet is your next stop. You'll just cross reference any company you are considering with any cards in the Never Again section to make sure you don't make that mistake twice.

WRITE TOOL

My handwriting is virtually illegible, and I have no patience for writing longhand.

I once tried calligraphy...for about three minutes.

However, I can type anything on the computer and change it to whatever font I like. And everybody can read it.

- I buy the small packs of printable file-folder labels because they are quick to make and much cheaper than anything that comes out of a label-making machine.

- I use sheets of clear address labels for my holiday cards. I only have to enter the addresses once. Each year, I update the list and print out the labels using an attractive font. This lets me spend more time making almost readable, personalized notes inside the cards, while the mailing addresses are neat and legible. The clear labels look nicer than the more industrial white labels, and I make sure to include a return address label with our family name so people will know that it isn't junk mail.

- I keep a file of favorite recipes I've downloaded, plus I type up a few old favorites whenever I get a couple of minutes and want to do something productive. I can choose a typeface and size that I find easy to read.

- I created a personal grocery list based on the aisle setup of my neighborhood grocery store. I can fit two lists on one page. I just print out a couple of pages, cut them in half and keep them handy.

- When the kids were little and I had to go out of town, I would type up a detailed itinerary for the person who would be staying with them. Not only did the itinerary include all of my contact information right at the top, but it clearly outlined the kids' normal routines for morning, after school, and evening. I also included menus that I had planned ahead. I would bind all the information in a little folder and make sure I inserted a letter of instruction and a copy of our health insurance coverage in the event of an emergency.

- I pay most of my bills online and never have to worry about writing a check, having stamps, or making sure the address appears in the window.

MAGIC MARKERS

I have a love/hate relationship with Sharpies®. You know, the amazing permanent markers that will write on almost anything?

Actually, I love them more than I hate them, and the only time I don't love them is when they've made it into the hands of a child. The usual result being one of the following:

- a trip to the home store for death primer and a new coat of paint for the wall (although doors have been the favored graffiti spot in my home);
- a requiem mass for a beloved outfit;
- an illegible phone/electric/credit card bill;
- days of humiliating explanations about your child's (or your) new "tattoo" until the skin finally sloughs away.

On the other hand, there aren't many things that you can have on hand that are so handy. They're great for labeling almost everything.

- All those wonderful storage containers we keep buying to get organized are simply more useful if you label the contents right on the container.
- How else would you label backpacks and book bags? (For safety, write the label behind the strap or inside the bag.)
- In the kitchen, I use a Sharpie® to note the date I put something in a freezer bag before I chunk it into the freezer. It's also handy for noting, right on the container, the date I opened the ubiquitous bottle of juice or soymilk—you know, those things that say use within five or ten days. By day four, I surely don't remember when I opened the darned thing. This way, I don't have to guess.

- I use them to label the spines of my three-ring binders.
- I like to use a red Sharpie® Pen to mark the important dates on the calendar that hangs in the kitchen. Once dry, it doesn't smear like a regular pen can.
- I keep one in my makeup drawer to keep track of my mascara's "discard" date. Mascara should be replaced every three to four months. I just write the discard date on the tube when I open a new one.
- I keep a red fine point near the washing machine to distinguish between my husband and son's jeans. The jeans look the same, but are different sizes. Rather than look at the labels for every pair, I draw a number one inside the double seam on the back of my husband's jeans and a two for my son's jeans.
- Although I try to change the filter in the air conditioner on a regular basis, I usually don't remember when I did it last. I solved this problem by marking the date on the side of the filter when I insert it into the unit.
- But my very favorite marker is the silver metallic Sharpie®. I use it to label all those annoying black phone chargers and power adapters. I used to waste time trying to guess which adapter charges which cell phone, or powers the calculator or the hand vac. The silver Sharpie® has saved me that frustration.

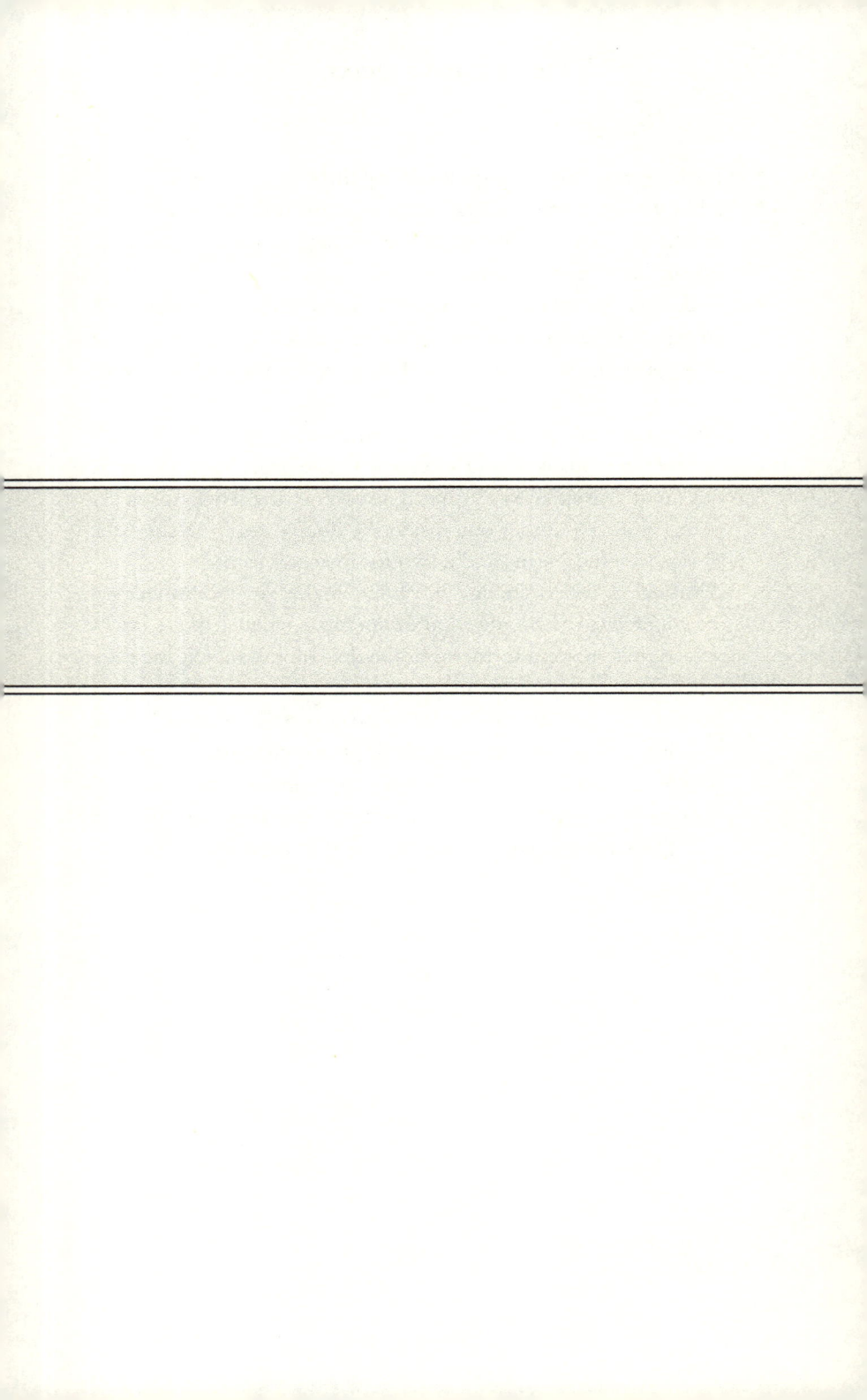

READY PACKS

Gear Up

A PLACE FOR EVERYTHING

When you are on the job 24/7, anything that wastes your time is simply unacceptable.

I have found that the biggest culprit of all is the time I've wasted looking for something I need, I know I have, but I just can't find. This drives me crazy. I have cut down on a lot of these hunting expeditions through the use of kits, or "ready packs."

The inspiration came when my sister-in-law, Sharon, and I were researching and writing *The Hurricane Handbook: A Practical Guide for Residents of the Hurricane Belt*. We generated varied lists of useful items based on hurricane preparations for families. I found that I could extend this concept to everyday activities and projects. The key is to keep the collected items together and contained so that you simply go to the appropriate ready pack to put your hand on just what you need. Some packs are pretty obvious; others are less so.

Getting started is simple. With the list in hand, gather the items that you *already have*. Set these on a countertop or table, and determine what kind of container will work for what you already have *plus* the items you want to add over time. You will probably be surprised, as I was, by how many of the items on your list you already own, but they were buried in a closet or drawer.

This simple exercise will actually save money in the long run because you won't find yourself "replacing" items you have but can't find. Print your own list of items for each pack and keep it in the container. Adjust the list as needs change, and use it to keep track of when it's time to replace an item.

Generally, I find that my favorite containers are clear, plastic, shoe boxes from a discount store. The containers are a very convenient size, you can immediately tell what's inside, and they stack for efficient storage.

WHAT IF?

The Packs Every Family Must Have

Consider the following list of disasters.

- Fires
- Tornadoes
- Earthquakes
- Floods
- Blizzards
- Gas leaks
- Chemical spills
- Hurricanes
- Acts of Terror

What does this list have to do with you? Everything! Disasters and accidents happen, usually with little or no warning. And when you watch news reports of people who have experienced these emergencies, there is always the sound bite, "I never thought this could happen to me." But it happens to *somebody* almost every day.

So, in addition to all the other hats you wear as a Domestic Commando, I am going to add one more: contingency planner. This is actually a real job. Businesses hire these professionals to imagine the worst and to *prepare* for it. As chief operating officer of your family, you must do the same. Imagine the worst, and do your best to prepare for it.

Now, I know the temptation is to say, "There is no way I can prevent any of these events." That's true. But what if they did happen to you? With a little preparation, you *can* influence how you respond to a crisis and how well your family comes out on the other side.

By planning and preparing, you can assume some *control* over your situation and make a difference.

With this in mind, there are a couple of packs that deserve special attention. They can directly impact the health and safety of family and home. If you do nothing else, PLEASE prepare a basic version of these packs. They will be welcome comfort whether you experience a simple power outage or a full-fledged emergency.

Special Note:

If anyone in your family depends on life-saving medications or equipment (remember the senior members of the family, as well), plan for this in advance. Your local pharmacy also may be affected by an event and may not be able to service requests for awhile.

Preferring to be as self-sufficient as possible, I like to have no less than a three-week supply of critical medicines on hand. This can be an issue with certain insurance policies. By considering this possibility ahead of time, you may realize that evacuation to an unaffected area may be a necessary part of your family's emergency plans.

THE DOCUMENTS PACK

When my sister-in-law and I did our research for *The Hurricane Handbook*, we interviewed dozens of people who had experienced major hurricanes. We were careful not to ask just the standard questions but to listen to what the "experts" had to say about what they did right and what they would do differently. We learned so much from so many people who generously shared their stories with us.

One of the most important things we learned about being ready for *any* emergency or disaster actually surprised us. And it costs nothing to do.

You need to have your documents in order. As a Domestic Commando, this is one of the most important things you can do for your family.

No single item will be more important for long-term recovery after an emergency or disaster than the Documents Pack. It is not glamorous. It is not attractive. It is not exciting. But it is essential! Most people would have to search through a couple of file cabinets, closets, and drawers to lay their hands on even one of these papers, let alone the entire bunch. Just imagine trying to do this in an emergency.

Be patient. You won't find everything in one day, but you will experience a real sense of accomplishment and relief when you have finished assembling your Documents Pack.

You may choose to keep most of these documents in a safe deposit box. It's important to have copies, at the very least, in an expandable file in a safe place at home. Store it in a waterproof container. It's also a good idea to scan these and keep them on a thumb drive or CD-ROM.

- [ ] birth certificates
- [ ] passports
- [ ] drivers' licenses*
- [ ] marriage license
- [ ] Social Security cards
- [ ] voter registration card
- [ ] health insurance cards
- [ ] insurance policies:
  - o homeowners/renters
  - o auto
  - o boat
  - o life insurance
- [ ] deed/lease
- [ ] mortgage
- [ ] property tax statement
- [ ] vehicle titles
- [ ] legal documents (wills, trusts, medical directives)
- [ ] backup copy of essential home/business computer files, especially financial data
- [ ] emergency cash stash—ATMs and even credit cards may not work if power is out or phone lines are down.

*Make sure your identification has your current address. In the event your family must evacuate, you will probably have to prove you live in the area before officials will let you return.

THE FIRST AID PACK

The inspiration for the First Aid Pack came when my sister-in-law moved to a house with no medicine cabinets in the bathrooms. She collected her first aid items in a container she stored out of reach of her kids.

I found the system extremely practical. Bathrooms are actually one of the worst places for medicines, due to the heat and humidity. Since the pack was so portable, I could just grab it and go. I tried keeping it in several spots around the house. In our home, the laundry room off the kitchen turned out to be the most functional spot.

I use a large tackle box from a sporting goods superstore. (You won't believe how many different variations of tackle boxes are available. One of them is sure to work for you.) The one I use has an outside section where I store bandages, antibiotic creams, anti-itch treatments—stuff I usually need quickly. Most everything else fits inside.

I also ended up outfitting a smaller tackle box to take on car trips with the kids. I learned to do this after spending a very long night in a small town with a small pharmacy and a sick child who would only take the kind of medicine we had at home. While this sounds ridiculously doting, familiarity is very comforting, especially when you don't feel well. It's a simple solution that takes very little effort.

Keep a list of the contents in the pack. Anything that has an expiration date should be noted for timely replacement.

Remember, you probably already have most of these items. Containerize them for convenience and add to it when needed items go on sale.

- list of contents and a pen to note expiration dates
- thermometer
- anti-biotic cream or ointment
- bandages (a variety of sizes and shapes)
- non-stick pads for large scrapes
- gauze rolls
- first aid tape
- scissors
- tweezers
- cotton swabs/cotton balls
- elastic knee brace and ankle brace
- triangular bandage for an arm sling
- measuring spoon or cup for liquid medicines
- eye dropper
- Betadine®
- hydrogen peroxide. (This is my favorite way to clean a scraped knee. Pour right onto the scrape. It will bubble and disinfect the area and provides a nice distraction.)
- anti-itch cream
- after-bite bug bite stick
- sun block
- eye wash
- eye drops
- ear drops
- anti-fungal cream
- pain relievers (adult and child versions)
- antacids
- allergy tablets
- cough and cold medicine
- throat lozenges
- laxative
- diarrhea medicine
- syrup of ipecac
- first aid book

THE EMERGENCY PACK

The list for the Emergency Pack seems daunting—and expensive—at first glance. But truthfully, you probably already have many of these items. They are just scattered everywhere.

The container for the Emergency Pack will need to be fairly large. But you must pick one that you can move on your own, and will fit in the trunk of your car if you must evacuate. If necessary, get two smaller containers and split the contents in whatever manner works for you.

My favorite place to look for an appropriate container is in the tool box section of a home-improvement store. These are built to be sturdy and often have internal storage for smaller items. They usually have handles, and some even come with built-in wheels.

I store my Emergency Pack in the front-entry closet. A well-protected interior closet or a shelf in the basement also are good spots. If your home has more than one floor, keep extra flashlights on each level so that you don't have to make your way in the dark to your Emergency Pack.

- ☐ flashlights (at least one for each member of the family, all using the same battery size)
- ☐ spare batteries
- ☐ battery-operated radio
- ☐ battery-operated lantern with spare batteries and bulbs (It provides general lighting, which is comforting to children and adults.)
- ☐ pillar candles*
- ☐ grill lighter
- ☐ can opener
- ☐ multi-tool or pocket knife

- ☐ work gloves
- ☐ safety goggles
- ☐ duct tape
- ☐ plastic sheeting and/or tarps
- ☐ contractor bags
- ☐ hammers
- ☐ nails

- ☐ space blankets
- ☐ insect repellant
- ☐ sun block
- ☐ camera (to take pictures of damage for insurance purposes)

*Please note that I only include candles in the event of a temporary power outage, and then, only the fat, pillar type that are more stable than a taper candle. Emergency workers have told me of cases where fires have started as a result of candle usage after a natural disaster. Debris on the roadways prevented the arrival of emergency services, creating a disaster within a disaster.

EVACUATION PACK

In the event you and your family need to evacuate, you will want additional items at the ready, especially if you end up in a shelter. It will make a real difference in how well you are able to cope. Think of this as a camping trip and you will be on the right track.

- ☐ Documents Pack
- ☐ prescription medications*
- ☐ First Aid Pack
- ☐ spare glasses/contacts
- ☐ baby wipes
- ☐ diapers
- ☐ feminine supplies
- ☐ tissues
- ☐ toilet paper
- ☐ travel-size toiletries
- ☐ pillows
- ☐ blankets/sleeping bags/air mattresses
- ☐ beach chairs
- ☐ towels
- ☐ small cooler
- ☐ favorite snacks and non-alcoholic drinks

*Any medications needed by any member of the family. Of course, you won't store these in the pack. Write a note on top of the container to remind you to gather these and carry them with you in the First Aid Pack. Take them in their original bottles so you have the prescription numbers, doses, etc.

Meanwhile, tell your kids, if they are old enough, that the family is going to make an adventure of the situation. Tell them to pack their own backpacks with activities and favorite items as though they would be on a deserted island for a few days. Be especially mindful of items your child needs to feel comforted or to sleep.

If your child is too young or is otherwise unable to do this on his or her own, make a basic list *now* of the backpack contents you will want to pack. It is virtually impossible to remember meaningful items under the pressure of an emergency. Tape the list to the top of the evacuation pack. Once you have the medicines collected, and *if there is still time*, grab the key items on the list and put them in your child's backpack.

HEIRLOOM BOX

Shortly after the sound bite when the disaster victim says she never thought this could happen to her family, there is the requisite shot of that same poor soul picking up a treasured memento that is now damaged or completely destroyed.

Hate is not a word I normally use, but it applies in this instance. I HATE seeing that person's pain and intruding on her sadness. Moreover, I feel awful for her loss.

This has inspired me to assemble a pack of treasures: things that really have no material value except that they are priceless to my family and me, and are truly irreplaceable. I call it the Heirloom Box. It can best be explained by example.

This is what my family's Heirloom Box contains:
- the outfits the children wore going home from the hospital;
- their baby books;
- their birth announcements;
- family videos;
- my father-in-law's baby book;
- a family bible;
- antique family pictures;
- our wedding album (many photographers hold the copyright to the pictures, so there may be no backup copies);
- my wedding planning book;
- scanned and backup copies of family photos (negatives, CD-ROMs and thumb drives);
- the annual calendars (you would be amazed at how much of our lives—vacations, parties, special events—are noted on these low-tech treasures);
- in a separate container, the family's holiday keepsakes.*

In other words, these are things that mean nothing to anyone else but mean *everything* to my family and me. This is the very simple criteria to determine what goes in.

Depending upon your situation and your home's layout, you may keep this in the entry closet to take with you in the event of an evacuation. If you have a basement, you might keep it down there on a high shelf. With the exception of a house fire, in which nothing is really safe, try to determine the safest spot for your Heirloom Box.

Finally, photograph or scan as many of these items as you can and store an extra set of digital copies along with digital photos in the safe deposit box where you keep your important documents.

*The holiday keepsakes include our annual, dated ornaments for the Christmas tree, the beautiful needlepoint stockings my mother-in-law made for each member of the family, the ornaments the children made at school, the ornaments we bought to commemorate when they were born, and the angel that tops the tree.

While the previous packs are absolute necessities, the following packs are about convenience. The lists are just suggestions. Simply adjust them to your own needs and preferences.

PURSE PACK

- ☐ small flashlight
- ☐ multi-tool (Hubby gave me a Leatherman® years ago that I still tote around.)
- ☐ phone
- ☐ wallet—the smallest possible
- ☐ lip gloss
- ☐ mirror
- ☐ comb

DIAPER BAG DAY PACK

This will fit in a very small bag and is really all you need to get through a day of errands.

- ☐ three or four diapers
- ☐ travel pack of wipes
- ☐ spare pacifier
- ☐ bottle of water
- ☐ small container of snacks, can of formula, or bottle of juice
- ☐ plastic zipper bags for diaper disposal

CAR PACK

- ☐ box of tissues
- ☐ pack of hard mints
- ☐ notepaper and pen (I always forget the note for the teacher until I am in the drop off line.)
- ☐ wet wipes for grimy faces and hands
- ☐ bandages
- ☐ feminine supplies (You or your daughter *will* be thankful.)
- ☐ spot-remover pads
- ☐ brush/comb
- ☐ ponchos/umbrella
- ☐ liquid hand disinfectant (Emergencies only. Overuse encourages resistant strains of bacteria and weakened immune systems.)
- ☐ floor mat or tarp to put under your child's chair when you go to someone else's home for dinner

MENDING PACK

- [ ] needles
- [ ] thread
  - black, white, and blue buttonhole thread will get you through most jobs
- [ ] snippers or small, sharp scissors
- [ ] thimble
- [ ] seam ripper
- [ ] box of buttons
  - miscellaneous white buttons are multi-purpose
  - buttons that come with new outfits should go right into this box
- [ ] iron-on patches
- [ ] iron-on hem tape
- [ ] liquid fray-stop

WRAPPING PACK

Dollar Tree® or a similar discount store is a great source for reasonably priced items.

- ☐ gift bags
- ☐ tissue stuffing
- ☐ pen or fine-point Sharpie®
- ☐ Instead of gift labels or cards, I buy (very cheap) corded tags from an office supply store. I "decorate" these with stamps, stickers or even sealing wax, and tie or tape them to the gift.

ART PACK

This is great to have on hand for a rainy day or for a play date.

- ☐ white paper
- ☐ colored construction paper
- ☐ boxes of crayons
- ☐ water color sets
- ☐ extra paint brushes/different shapes
- ☐ glass jars for water (Peanut butter jars are a good weight and height.)
- ☐ safety scissors
- ☐ miscellaneous stickers, stamps (Some junk mail is a great source of this stuff.)
- ☐ white paste
- ☐ washable markers
- ☐ colored pencils
- ☐ erasers
- ☐ old magazines with pictures to cut out for collages

MANUALS PACK

Store all owner's manuals for everything in one place. When you need to review how to drain the water heater, you will know exactly where to get the manual. I have found it convenient to use an expandable file or a portable file box for manuals storage.

- ☐ stove
- ☐ refrigerator
- ☐ washer/dryer
- ☐ freezer
- ☐ vacuum
- ☐ water heater
- ☐ AC/heating system
- ☐ TV/DVD/DVR/sound system, etc.
- ☐ sewing machine
- ☐ all small kitchen appliances

CRAFT PACK

Even the craft-challenged need some supplies

- ☐ glue gun (Where else would my hubby find it?)
- ☐ glue sticks
- ☐ scissors
- ☐ craft knife
- ☐ hole punch
- ☐ white glue
- ☐ white paper
- ☐ colored paper
- ☐ paint pens (white/silver/gold)
- ☐ decorative scissors
- ☐ stickers
- ☐ stamp pad and stamps
- ☐ scrapbooking goodies

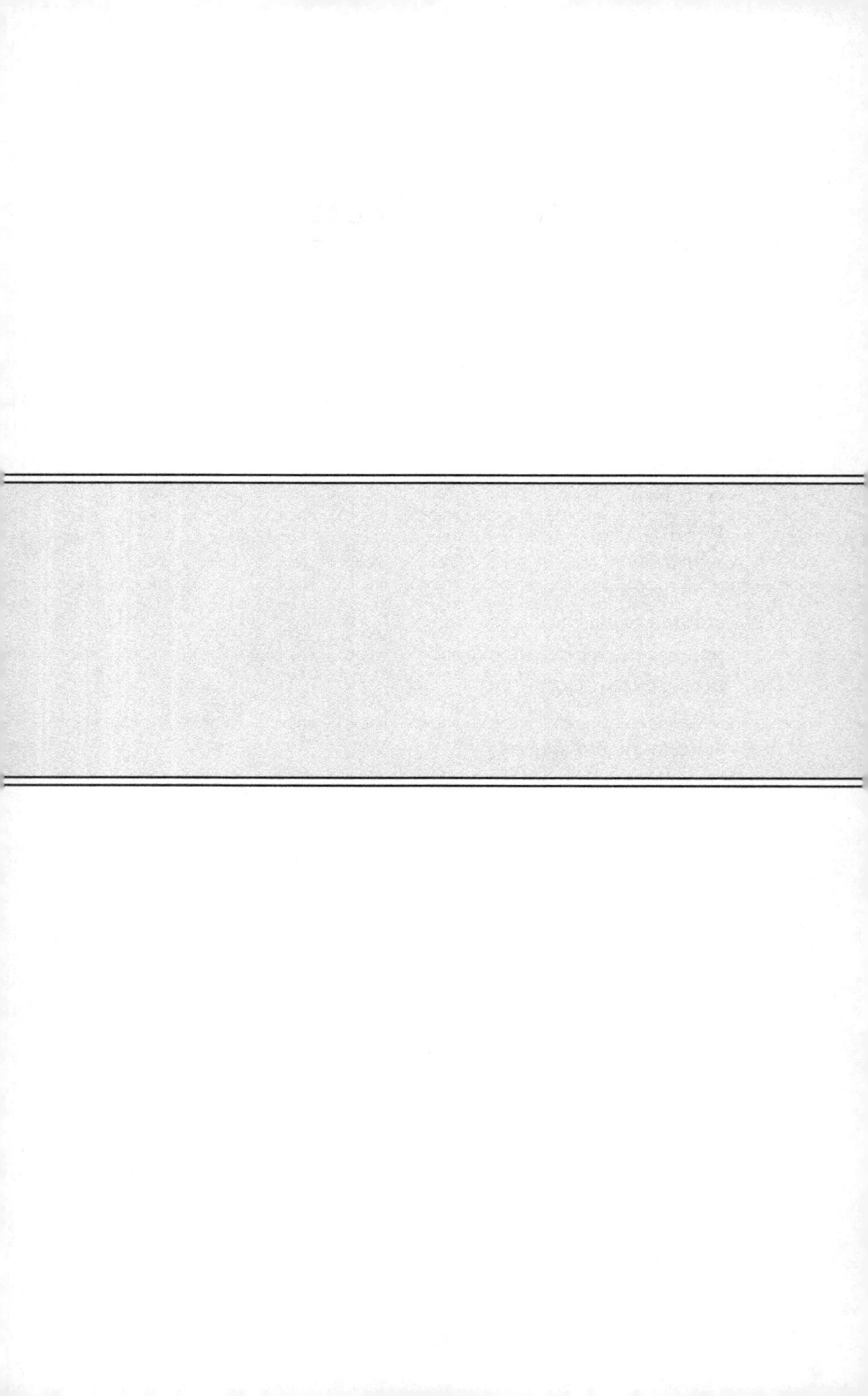

FEEDING THE TROOPS

KP Duty

KP CONFESSIONS

As noted earlier, I am craft-challenged. But that's okay because cooking is my favorite creative outlet. This preference goes back farther than I care to admit. I remember reading cookbooks for pleasure in college when I needed a break from my textbooks. Once the kids were in school, I was lucky enough to work as a freelance producer/director for a food show.

So, I began with the advantage of being a foodie. But there are so many reasons today to prepare your own meals. The first thing everyone thinks about is the savings. There is no question that cooking from scratch is far less expensive than buying prepared foods.

But for a Domestic Commando, there also is the benefit of quality control. You *know* what is going into the food you are serving your family. The closer the ingredients are to their natural state, the less "rubbish" (i.e. chemicals, fillers, dyes, high fructose corn syrup, etc.) is going into your family. Food labels should be read—by your kids, when they are old enough—as well as you. The simple rule I taught them was that if we couldn't pronounce an ingredient, it probably wasn't something we should eat. My daughter took this to heart and even counsels her friends to read food labels. My son? Not so much.

But perhaps the most valuable benefit to cooking at home is the foundation it provides the family. If you took the time to prepare a meal, the family should gather and share it together. It makes a difference. I will always remember the day my daughter came home after a sleepover and said, somewhat stunned, that her friend's mom doesn't cook. They just order out from one place or another. Then her friend takes her plate of takeout to her room to eat. My daughter realized how special family meals were to her, and was sorry that many of her friends didn't have this same experience.

In this section, I have included some tactics I have learned to make kitchen duty a little easier as well as some family recipes that are simple enough for weekday preparation or are so tasty, that they are worth the little extra time they take to prepare.

CULINARY QUIRKS

I cook with gas, so you may need to make adjustments if you cook on an electric stovetop.

I use the microwave mostly to defrost and to heat things through. I do not consider it a way to cook. That said, there simply is no better tool to reheat rice.

Microwave ovens have their own personalities, depending upon size and vintage. For this reason, I don't really give details of their use in the recipes and techniques that follow. You know your own appliance. When in doubt, use half power for a minute or two (depending on the size and density of the dish you are heating) and check before zapping again.

I don't care for store-bought chicken broth. I find it bland and don't like the color. If I don't have homemade broth, I substitute Swanson's Vegetable Broth (the one in the carton) whenever a recipe calls for broth or stock. I love the deeper color and flavor. The Better than Broth concentrate in the jar (vegetable flavor) is also an acceptable substitute. It doesn't have the monosodium glutamate (MSG) found in some bouillon products, and is much more affordable than the Swanson's broth.

Beans and rice are to me what meat and potatoes are to most people. This turned out to be a good thing, because I don't eat a lot of meat and never really have. I do cook meat dishes for my family, but if a steak is involved, Hubby does the honors. I can't help but overcook it every time.

My mother was born in Cuba. She could cook rice in her sleep, and so can I. Use long grain, white rice. Don't use parboiled rice, as it doesn't have the fluffy texture of regular rice. I don't think it soaks up the flavors of sauces and beans, either. The key to making rice is to use the same measuring cup for the rice and the water. You will use exactly twice as much liquid as rice. Add salt and a little oil or butter, if you like. Cover the pot and bring to a boil. Reduce the heat to the lowest setting on your stove and simmer for seventeen to twenty minutes. *Never* remove the lid to peek or stir until the time is up. You will release the steam that is crucial to making tender, fluffy rice.

I believe everyone should have a kitchen garden. I have had good success growing my favorite herbs in containers. I buy the seedlings in the four-inch pots at the home-improvement store early in the season and transplant them to larger pots with fresh potting soil. I have had good luck growing basil, rosemary, thyme, flat leaf parsley, chives, and oregano. Admittedly, I haven't had much success with cilantro. It usually turns yellow and dies a few weeks after transplanting. But I usually get one or two good batches of salsa served up before that happens.

I use only kosher salt for cooking. I buy the flake-style salt from Penzeys Spices. It has the coarse texture I prefer. I buy it in the bulk package and transfer it to a glass storage jar. For everyday cooking, I keep a small portion in a ceramic bowl by the stove and season my recipes one pinch at a time.

I believe you should buy the best knives you can afford. There is no point in scrimping here because a good set will last for years. Quality stainless steel is a must. I like the handle to have good weight and balance and should not slip if your hands are damp. The four basic knives I must have are an eight-inch chef's knife, a bread knife, a paring knife, and a Santoku knife.

I only have one non-stick pan, which I use for cooking eggs. Everything else is cooked in a stainless steel pot or pan. I don't really like using non-stick at all because it has been known to release toxic gasses (strong enough to kill pet birds), but I hate leaving half my eggs burned on the bottom of a pan. Of course, if I could properly maintain a well-seasoned iron skillet, I would be better off. But I can't stop myself from washing the skillet—which, of course, ruins the "well-seasoned" character.

The criteria for any recipe should be how delicious, nutritious and do-able the dish is—not how many hoops you have to jump through to get it to the table.

When we make hamburgers, there is always a small, unseasoned patty for the dog. He is a wonderful dog.

PICK-PICK-PICK

Getting kids to eat "real" food (i.e., food that an adult would want to eat because it actually has flavor) can be a daunting challenge.

It seems that the seasonings are often the biggest problem. I found the best way around this is to apply the principle of big and little ingredients. Either cut them so small they can't be noticed, or cut them big enough that the child can pick them out. The latter technique works well for items like bell peppers.

On the other hand, one of my children objects to onions. But some recipes, particularly soups, just *need* onions. I found the best way to hide the onions is to grate them on a box grater. This produces a juicy onion sauce that's surprisingly strong. So you'll need less onion than the recipe calls for. (Note that it won't work for a recipe that depends on browned or caramelized onions. Too much heat and the onion juice just burns.)

This simple principle has been a pretty effective way to reach some level of compromise between my adult preference for full-flavored foods and the need to feed a picky eater.

FAIRY-TALE BREAKFAST

Feeding my kids was often little more than a name game.

When it came to breakfast, I found the word *porridge* to be a useful tool. After all, the Three Bears liked it. More importantly, the term porridge could be applied to any hot cereal. So we had oatmeal porridge, Cream of Wheat® porridge, and of course, grit porridge. I would prepare variations on each of these.

I preferred Cream of Wheat® porridge with butter only. But my kids also liked it with jelly swirled on top (ugh!) or grated cheddar. Cheese grits was the preferred version of grits.

Oatmeal porridge was always made with the five-minute variety of oatmeal. I find instant oatmeal is too gooey (the kids didn't mind) and the one-minute variety is still a little too mealy for my taste.

Because I like some "bite" to my oatmeal, I usually begin with two-thirds to three-fourths the amount of water the recipe calls for. When the water begins to boil, I add the salt and the oats. Stir, reduce the heat, and set the timer for five minutes. I may give it a quick stir a couple more times while I'm preparing the toast. When the porridge has about two minutes to go, I check to see if it's getting too thick (usually not) and may add a splash of water.

Oatmeal porridge is normally served with a little butter, milk, brown sugar, and vanilla. It's also great with chopped apples and walnuts. We called this version "school oatmeal" because it was heartier for all that hard work to be done. I had one child who actually enjoyed this version for several years.

FOUR MEALS AND A SIDE

When good, lean, ground beef is on sale, it's time to grill burgers with a bonus.

I think burgers made from frozen ground beef are just too tough. So I like to use fresh ground beef. Since Hubby will be doing the grilling, I take the opportunity to save myself some work down the line.

This tactic was inspired by a variety of books that show you how to prepare batches of meals just once or twice a month and store them in your freezer. I tried this system a couple of times and found that it just wasn't for me. I enjoy cooking and this was simply too regimented. Plus, I was completely depressed by the mountain of pans to be washed at the end of the day. But some days you just want a homemade dish that's virtually ready to go. So this is my mini-version of batch cooking. Frankly, the recipe doesn't matter; this is really about procedure. It also has the advantage of running your oven only once for triple duty.

I buy five and a half to six pounds of lean ground beef.

Meal 1:

I make four hamburgers (plus the small one), a little larger than the size of the hamburger buns we will be using. I make sure they are not too thick because my kids like them pretty well done and it is hard to cook a thick burger all the way through. This will usually take over a pound of the meat (for some reason, that quarter-pound concept never works out with homemade burgers). I set these on a platter lined with wax paper and season them according to each family member's preference. Hubby starts heating the gas grill about this time, giving the hamburgers some time to marinate.

Meal 2:

I take about a pound of ground beef, gently form it into a patty, and wrap it for the freezer. This will be thawed and used in tacos, chili, *picadillo* (a savory Cuban meat dish), or any recipe that calls for browned ground beef.

Meals 3 and 4:

I pull off about a quarter of the remaining ground beef and set it aside, leaving about two and a half to three pounds, which go into a large mixing bowl. I make a well in the center. I crack two eggs into the well and beat them with a fork. Next, I add the ingredients for my favorite meat loaf recipe—basically, milk, bread crumbs, and various seasonings, adjusting the amounts for the quantity of meat I'm using. I gently mix the ingredients into the ground beef, trying not to overwork the beef. I line a shallow baking pan with foil and oil the top of the foil. Next, I form two meat loaves and set them onto the foil. I actually prefer using a sheet pan instead of loaf pans because it prevents the meatloaves from sitting in a puddle of grease. These go into a 375° oven for about an hour, or until there is no pink in the middle. I just poke and peek with a paring knife. Remove and cool. Wrap them and freeze.

Defrost meatloaf overnight or in the microwave the next day. Heat in a small, glass casserole pan until hot. You can do this in the oven, toaster oven, or microwave. You should only need to heat it through because the meat is already cooked. Just before serving, top with gravy or marinara sauce.

The "side":

I season and form the remaining ground beef into meatballs. Again, the recipe doesn't matter, the process is the point. Form the meatballs and set them onto another small, foil-lined pan that has been oiled. Pop them into the oven with the meatloaves. Turn them over in about fifteen minutes and bake for another ten minutes. Cool and pop into a zipper bag and freeze. These defrost in a couple of minutes in most microwaves. Heat them gently and sauce them with some of your favorite pasta sauce. A quick and easy way to beef up a pasta dish.

THE WORLD IS NOT FLAT, BUT MY CHICKEN IS

I have found a method for roasting a whole chicken that gives me great results every time.

Normally, when I pull a whole chicken out of the oven, I find portions where the juices just don't run clear even though the majority of the bird is cooked through. The simple solution is to roast the chicken FLAT. Simply take the chicken to the meat counter and ask the butcher to cut the back bone out of the chicken. You also can do this yourself at home with a decent pair of poultry shears, being careful of the sharp bones through which you will be cutting. When you get home, open the bird to lay skin-side-up on the rack of your roasting pan. Push down on the breast bone to crack it and you have a perfectly flat, whole chicken to roast. Slather the chicken with olive oil, garlic salt, and thyme, or your favorite seasonings. Roast about an hour in a 375° oven.

To get a one-pan meal out of your flat-roasted chicken, cut up some washed creamer potatoes and carrots, and place them in the bottom of the roasting pan. Toss them with olive oil, salt, pepper, and garlic, then position the rack with the flattened chicken right on top. The chicken will share its drippings with the vegetables, making an incredibly delicious (and unabashedly simple) meal.

Collect the backbones from your flattened roaster in a freezer bag. When you have five or six backbones, thaw them and place them in a roasting pan with whole, washed carrots, potatoes, celery, onions, and a head of garlic. Drizzle everything with olive oil, and season with salt and pepper. Roast in a 375° oven for about an hour. Transfer everything except the roasted garlic to a stock pot and cover with water. Add a few whole, peeled cloves of garlic to the stock pot and simmer, lightly covered, about forty-five minutes, or until the stock looks and smells rich and tasty (forty-five minutes to an hour—this isn't an exact science). Drain the stock through a colander, cool, and skim off the fat. Transfer to a freezer container or two. Meanwhile, cut the top off the whole, roasted garlic and squeeze the paste from the clove pockets onto some toast. Yum!

KITCHEN TACTICS

When grocery shopping, I set all my cold items on the checkout belt first and have these bagged together. (Raw meats get their own bag.) Dry goods are then bagged separately. When I get home, I can easily unload all the cold items first. The dry goods can wait on the counter if someone or something needs my attention.

For ease of preparation and quality of flavor, I really love Duncan® Hines cookie mixes. They take no time to prepare and I find the flavor is fuller than the refrigerated dough. But I do like the convenience of those little logs of goodness. When I mix up a batch of cookies, I only bake about a dozen at a time—enough for three or four cookies per person. The remaining dough is plopped onto a piece of plastic wrap or wax paper, formed into a log, and wrapped in the plastic. I give this a final wrap with aluminum foil and pop it into the freezer (make a note of the baking temperature with indelible marker right on the foil). I can bake up two or three more batches by slicing off a hunk from the log with a stout knife and popping the rest back into the freezer. In the time it takes to preheat the oven, the dough is soft enough to divide into cookies on your cookie sheet. Fresh-baked cookies every time!

My mother didn't have written recipes or a crock pot. She just had a pressure cooker and a wide variety of dried beans in the cupboard. There was always some kind of bean soaking in a bowl overnight in the kitchen. The next morning, she would drain the beans and pop them into the pressure cooker with her favorite seasonings. Basically, dinner would be ready by midday so she didn't have to stress over preparations at the end of the day. Furthermore, a bag of dried beans always made enough extra to freeze for future dinners. It was an extremely efficient use of time and energy.

Sautéing or searing chicken breasts in a pan can be tricky because the full part of the breast takes so much longer to cook than the "tail" end. To solve this problem, butterfly the breasts before you season and cook them. They cook more evenly and much faster, which also means they won't be so dry.

In a pinch, roasted chickens from the grocery store are a perfectly acceptable way to get a head start on a recipe that calls for cooked chicken. While it is generally less expensive to roast your own whole chicken, occasionally my local store runs a sale on roasted chickens which actually turns out to be cheaper.

I like using fresh breadcrumbs whenever I can. I just tear up the ends of the current loaf of bread (and maybe one or two extra slices), toss these into the blender and give it a whir. I especially like to use fresh crumbs in meat loaf, as it seems to produce a more tender result.

I rarely use Parmesan cheese. I normally substitute pecorino Romano, which is slightly less expensive than a quality Parmesan and has much more intense flavor. I think it just gives more bang for the buck.

I cook bacon in the oven. I love it because the bacon stays flat, cooks up crisp, and it is infinitely less messy. I cook half a package at a time. The remaining half is covered with plastic wrap and popped into the freezer. I will lay the half pack of frozen bacon on a paper towel, on a microwave-safe plate and zap it for about two minutes to make it easier to separate the slices. I line a shallow baking pan with aluminum foil and lay the slices in a single layer. I pop this into a cold oven. I turn the oven on to 350°. When my oven reaches temperature, it beeps and I remove the bacon. With tongs, I turn all the pieces over and pop the pan back into the oven. I check the bacon after another five minutes, and then every one or two minutes after that. I use a kitchen timer so I don't forget if I become distracted with something else. When crispy, I transfer the bacon to several layers of paper towels to drain. I usually pour the bacon drippings into an old can and toss the aluminum foil.

No matter how much you cajole or threaten, you may not be successful at getting your kids to eat cooked vegetables at meal time. It is perfectly reasonable, definitely healthier, and certainly less wasteful, to set out cut up fruits and vegetables rather than elaborate sides or salads. It takes almost no time to:

- slice an apple or pear, rub the slices with a lemon wedge and top with a small piece of cheese;
- cut an orange into wedges;
- slice a banana into chucks, toss in a little orange juice, and top with a few chopped nuts and raisins;
- cube available fruit into a bowl for fruit salad; (Top with a drizzle of honey, or a light dressing of plain yogurt that you've flavored with honey and a small bit of lime zest.)
- lightly steam batches of carrots, broccoli, or green beans. Chill and serve with ranch dressing at dinner time. (It's good for snacking, as well.)

My favorite kitchen centerpiece is a basket with a mix of fresh, seasonal fruits. If it is sitting right in front of you, it's much easier to train your kids (and yourself) to grab and peel a piece of fresh fruit when the urge to snack hits.

I prefer golden raisins to the traditional dark raisins. They always seem plumper and mildly sweet. Children who normally object to raisins will sometimes accept these instead.

I know a woman who unabashedly declares that peanut butter will sustain life. I'm not sure I can disagree with her. However, I have become something of a peanut butter snob. I really only like the "natural" peanut butters. Nothing's added but a little salt. They also have a texture far superior to the homogenized versions, especially the crunchy style. The only fault I can find with natural peanut butter is that you have to stir in the oil that separated out while the jar sat on the shelf. This was a messy proposition at best, until my hubby was faced with a new jar of peanut butter. He simply transferred everything into a mixing bowl, stirred it all together and transferred it back to the jar. If you use a silicon spoon for the transfer, you can get virtually every bit of peanut butter back into the jar.

Fight the temptation to refrigerate tomatoes. Tomatoes undergo a chemical reaction when temperatures dip below 50° that actually robs the tomato of its flavor. If you've ever grown tomatoes, you know how true this is.

To slice a tomato for a sandwich, turn the flat, stem end down onto your cutting board, and then slice straight down. These "sideways" slices spread more of the flesh throughout each slice, which make them less watery. Yes, they look different, but they're going to be *inside* the sandwich anyway!

When shopping for tomatoes, consider buying the little, oval Roma tomatoes instead of the typical, round salad tomatoes. They often have a better price per pound, are meatier than salad tomatoes, and taste just as good (sometimes better).

Cubanelle peppers are an excellent, and less expensive, alternative to green bell peppers. The peppers are not hot and they have a milder flavor than the bell peppers. The skin is thinner and the pieces cook up nice and tender.

Never underestimate the power of a crinkle cutter (it has a blade with wavy edges) to get your child to try a vegetable with some dip. It works great on zucchini, carrots, yellow squash and even sweet bell peppers. Cut the slices very thinly for best texture. You also can dress up a cheese plate by using the cutter to slice and cube blocks of cheese.

Changing the texture also can work to get kids to try zucchini and carrots.

- Coarsely grate zucchini. Place it on a couple of paper towels or on a clean kitchen towel and gently squeeze out the excess moisture. In a large skillet over medium heat, gently sauté the zucchini in butter seasoned with a couple of cloves of garlic. When the zucchini begins to wilt (three to five minutes), season with some salt to taste. The salt will draw additional moisture from the zucchini. Turn the heat up slightly to gently cook off most of this moisture (another three to five minutes) and serve.
- To prepare shredded carrots, coarsely grate the carrots. Over medium heat, sauté the carrots in butter with a little salt to taste. When the carrots are just tender (five to seven minutes) add a splash of orange juice. Heat gently for just a minute and serve.

Use an inexpensive sandwich bag to quickly and cleanly grease or butter a pan. Slide your hand into the bag and use it like a plastic mitten. The warmth of your fingers makes short work of spreading the butter and you can still get it into tight spaces.

I love wax paper. It's inexpensive and versatile, and I try never to run out of it. Here are a few ways it makes my life easier.

- Form a funnel with a square of wax paper and use it to transfer dry ingredients into a small-mouthed container.
- When you're grilling, line the meat platter with a couple of layers of wax paper. After the meats go onto the grill, throw the wax paper away and you have a clean platter ready to receive your cooked meats, minus the cross-contamination.

- This same approach can be used to protect your countertops from contamination after cleaning and cutting meats for a stovetop recipe.
- Tape a few sheets of wax paper onto a work table with masking tape to make an art mat for kids. Although butcher paper would be a first choice, it's more expensive and isn't always as available.
- I prefer to use wax paper to cover dishes in the microwave rather than plastic wrap. Because it doesn't seal tightly, it vents naturally; and I don't like the way plastic wrap feels almost melted when you pull the hot dish out of the microwave.
- When measuring dry ingredients for baking, spoon your flour, sugar, etc. into your measuring cup over a sheet of wax paper. Use a knife or spatula to level the excess right onto the wax paper. Lift the edges of the paper and pour excess dry ingredient back into its container. (This procedure is especially effective when little helpers are learning to cook in the kitchen. There's far less mess, virtually no waste, and it makes it easy for them to learn how to clean up).

BASIC RICE

This recipe is good to serve with beans, Chinese food, even fried eggs.

If you want to serve the rice as a side dish, substitute vegetable broth for half the water.

2-3 teaspoons butter
1½ cups long grain, regular white rice
3 cups water
1 teaspoon salt

1. Sauté the rice in the butter in a medium saucepan over medium-high heat, being careful not to burn it.
2. When the rice grains start turning white, add the water and salt. (Be careful, the water will steam up when it hits the hot pan.)
3. Cover the pot and bring to a boil.
4. Turn the heat down to the lowest setting possible and cook for 17 to 20 minutes. Do not peek—you want to preserve the steam in the pot to get the fluffiest rice possible. When the surface of the rice is dotted with little holes, it is probably done.
5. Fluff with a fork and serve.

OVEN-BAKED PILAF

An interesting recipe, as the rice is not cooked on the stove top. Great for company. The original recipe from my mother-in-law called for double the butter, but that was too much for my taste.

¼ cup butter
2 cups uncooked rice
2 teaspoons salt
2 (14-ounce) cans beef broth
½ cup blanched almonds

1. Cook rice in butter over medium-high heat until golden.
2. Add other ingredients and transfer to a covered casserole dish.
3. Bake at 325° for 75 minutes.

NANA'S BEST CHICKEN CASSEROLE

This was one of my mother-in-law's signature dishes. I have never met anyone who didn't go back for seconds. She usually served it with a spoonful of guava or currant jelly on the side.

This may be one of the world's great comfort dishes. It is perfect to take to a family with a new baby or to share with a family that is grieving. Prepare it in a foil pan, so they don't have to worry about returning it. Don't forget to include instructions for defrosting and heating.

Note: My mother-in-law made this recipe with a whole chicken. I usually use chicken breasts. You can't go wrong either way.

1 large chicken (about 4 pounds) or 5-6 chicken breast halves
1 stick butter
1 (8-ounce) package Pepperidge Farm® Herb Seasoned Stuffing
1 can cream of chicken soup (condensed)
1¾ cup chicken broth, divided
1 cup sour cream

1. Cook chicken, allow it to cool, and remove meat from bones. For the tastiest chicken, oil the skin and roast it in the oven (a grocery store roasted chicken is perfectly fine, too).
2. Melt butter and mix with stuffing mix. Reserve one cup for topping later.
3. Spread remaining butter-and-stuffing mixture in bottom of a 3-quart casserole. Place cooked, cut-up chicken on top.
4. Mix soup, chicken broth and sour cream. Pour over chicken and stuffing.
5. Sprinkle reserved stuffing-and-butter mixture on top.

6. Dot with butter.
7. Drizzle another ¾ cup of broth on top to moisten.
8. Bake at 350° until hot, about 30 minutes.

This dish freezes fabulously. You can assemble two casseroles at one time and pop one into the oven while the other goes into the freezer. When your menu planning calls for this casserole, just thaw it and bake as directed.

3-STEP CHICKEN

It just doesn't get any easier than this.

8 chicken pieces
1 envelope onion soup mix
1 small bottle red Russian dressing
8-ounce jar apricot jam

1. Combine dry soup mix, Russian dressing, and jam. Mix well until there are no lumps.
2. Wash chicken and pat dry.
3. Place chicken pieces in a flat, oven-proof dish.
4. Spoon some sauce beneath and on top of skin for each piece of chicken.
5. Bake for 50-60 minutes in 375° oven. Juices should run clear.

The sauce can be prepared ahead of time and will keep very well in the refrigerator.

TURKEY TETRAZZINI

Something a little different for leftover Thanksgiving turkey.
You also can substitute diced, cooked chicken for the turkey.

4 tablespoons butter
¼ cup flour
2 cups stock
½ pound fresh mushrooms
2 tablespoons butter
½ pound spaghetti
2 tablespoons sherry
½ cup parmesan cheese
1 cup half-and-half
2½ cups diced, cooked turkey

1. Melt butter. Blend in flour. Cook 3 minutes.
2. Whisk in stock. Cook until smooth and thick.
3. Sauté mushrooms in 2 tablespoons butter until wilted.
4. Add sauce, sherry, half-and-half and turkey.
5. Cook spaghetti in boiling, salted water until tender. Drain.
6. Grease 8" x 12" baking dish. Pour in half of spaghetti.
7. Cover with half of turkey mixture.
8. Repeat. Sprinkle with cheese.
9. Bake at 350° for 30 minutes or until browned.

ISLAND CHICKEN

This recipe is a good example of using big ingredients that are easily removed for a picky eater while providing a fully flavored meal for adults.

2 large onions, sliced
1 green pepper (or Cubanelle) cut into large pieces
12 pieces of chicken—legs and thighs (about 2 per person)
1 (20–ounce) can of pineapple chunks, drained
1 bottle barbecue sauce

1. Spread onions and green pepper pieces over the bottom of a 13" x 9" casserole dish.
2. Arrange chicken pieces on top.
3. Sprinkle pineapple chunks over the chicken.
4. Pour barbecue sauce over all.
5. Cover with foil and put in 350° oven for two hours. Baste once or twice.
6. Pour off excess juice and put back in the oven to dry out and brown a little, another 10-15 minutes.

The chicken can remain in the oven for up to an hour, making it a good recipe for company.

POT ROAST

This recipe comes from my sister. The simple seasonings have an earthy quality that is the essence of comfort food. She makes it in a pot on the stove; I use a pressure cooker to speed things up. I have included both methods.

1/4 cup flour
2 teaspoons salt
1/4 teaspoon pepper
3 pounds chuck roast (I often use flank steak because it is leaner, but it's a little stringier.)
1 medium onion, chopped
1/8 cup olive oil
3 cups boiling water, divided
5-6 garlic cloves, chopped
1/4 teaspoon ground cumin
4-6 potatoes, peeled and quartered
3-4 carrots, scraped and cut into thirds

Stove-Top Method

1. Combine flour, salt and pepper.
2. Dredge meat in flour mixture.
3. Heat oil in pot over medium-high heat.
4. Add meat and onions to oil, brown meat on all sides.
5. Add garlic and cumin, and pour half of boiling water over all.
6. Cook gently on stove about 3 hours until meat is tender and falls apart. (Add hot water as necessary).
7. Add potatoes and carrots with the last cup of water during the last hour of cooking.

Pressure Cooker Method

1. Combine flour, salt and pepper.
2. Dredge meat in flour mixture.
3. Heat oil in pot over medium-high heat.
4. Add meat and onions to oil; brown meat on all sides.
5. Add garlic and cumin. Pour half of boiling water over all.
6. Cover and cook meat under pressure for 30 minutes.
7. Let cool until pressure is released.
8. Add potatoes, carrots, and remaining water.
9. Cook under pressure an additional 20 minutes.

In the winter, this is great served with some crusty bread or plain rice.

BEEF BAR B CUPS

¾ pound ground beef
½ cup barbecue sauce
2 tablespoons brown sugar
1 can refrigerator biscuits, regular size
¾ cup shredded cheddar cheese

1. In a large skillet, brown the ground beef and drain.
2. Add barbecue sauce and brown sugar.
3. Place each biscuit in an ungreased muffin cup, pressing dough up the sides to the edge of the cup.
4. Spoon meat into cups.
5. Bake at 400° for 10-15 minutes or until golden brown.
6. Sprinkle with cheese and serve.

OVEN-BAKED BEEF PATTIES

1 pound ground beef
½ cup packaged biscuit mix
⅓ cup tomato juice, V8® juice, etc.
¼ cup finely chopped green or Cubanelle pepper (optional)
1 slightly beaten egg
1 small clove garlic, minced
½ teaspoon oregano, crushed
Dash pepper
½ teaspoon Worcestershire
Shredded Romano cheese

1. Combine beef, biscuit mix, tomato juice, green pepper, egg, garlic, and seasoning. Mix lightly until blended.
2. Shape into four patties and place in greased, shallow baking pan.
3. Bake at 400° for 20 minutes. Remove from oven.
4. Sprinkle each patty with a couple of teaspoons of Romano cheese.

Serve with buttered noodles or potatoes.

TAMALE CASSEROLE

1 pound ground beef
½ cup sliced onions, (medium size)
1 (14-ounce) can of crushed tomatoes
½ cup ripe olives, coarsely chopped
1 (6-ounce) can tomato paste
1 tablespoon chili powder
1 teaspoon salt
½ cup chopped green pepper
1 ½ cups corn (frozen or canned)
1 small box "Jiffy" Corn Muffin Mix.

1. Mix ground beef with the onions and shape into a large patty. Brown 5 minutes on each side, then break into chunks.
2. Stir in tomatoes, sauce, and seasonings (*basically, everything else on the list except the muffin batter*)
3. Heat to boiling.
4. Prepare corn muffin mix according to package directions.
5. Spread half of the batter in the bottom of a greased baking dish.
6. Spoon in meat mixture.
7. Drop remaining batter by spoonfuls on top.
8. Bake at 375° for 35 minutes or until puffed and brown.

OVERNIGHT LAYERED SALAD

My hubby's absolute favorite. Great for a pot luck.

1 head lettuce
½ cup sliced onion
½ to 1 cup thinly sliced celery
1 can water chestnuts, drained
1 (10-ounce) package frozen peas, thawed and drained
2 cups mayonnaise
2 teaspoons sugar
½ cup grated Parmesan cheese
1 teaspoon seasoned salt
¼ teaspoon garlic powder
3 hard cooked eggs, sliced
½ to ¾ pound bacon, fried and crumbled

1. Remove the peas from the freezer and let them thaw while preparing the rest of the ingredients.
2. Chop lettuce and place in the bottom of a large bowl.
3. Top with layers of onion, celery, water chestnuts, and peas.
4. Spread mayonnaise evenly over top.
5. Sprinkle with sugar, Parmesan, salt, and garlic powder. Cover with plastic wrap.
6. Chill at least overnight for best results.
7. Before serving, toss and sprinkle with eggs and bacon.

GREEN BEAN AND BACON CASSEROLE

A good recipe for company, as the dish can be prepared ahead of time.

2 cans French-cut string beans (*or 1½ pounds fresh green beans, steamed or blanched*)
1 medium onion cut in rings
8 strips bacon
½ cups slivered almonds
6 tablespoons sugar
6 tablespoons red wine vinegar

1. Drain beans and put in 1½-quart casserole.
2. Place separated onion rings over beans.
3. Cook bacon and reserve drippings.
4. Cut bacon into quarters and lay over onion rings.
5. Sprinkle almonds over bacon.
6. Add sugar and vinegar to bacon drippings, and heat.
7. Pour over casserole.
8. Marinate several hours or overnight.
9. Bake at 350° for 45 minutes.

PECAN-TOPPED SWEET POTATOES

My mother-in-law's alternative to the "horror" of my childhood's marshmallow-topped sweet-potato casserole. Even my Southern family has come to enjoy this recipe.

6 cups cooked, mashed sweet potatoes
or
Peel, cube and steam 3½ to 4 pounds of yams, then mash
2 eggs
¾ cup brown sugar (or less)
½ cup butter, melted
1 teaspoon salt
1 teaspoon cinnamon
Orange Juice (up to 1 cup)
1 cup pecan halves

1. Mash potatoes.
2. Beat in eggs then half of the sugar, half of the butter, salt, and cinnamon.
3. If potatoes seem dry, beat in orange juice until light and fluffy.
4. Put in a 1½- or 2-quart buttered casserole.
5. Refrigerate if preparing ahead of time.
6. Before baking, arrange pecans on top.
7. Sprinkle with remaining sugar and drizzle with remaining butter.
8. Bake uncovered at 375° for 20 minutes or until heated through.

HERBED CRACKERS

Supposedly, this recipe keeps fresh a long time. We have no way of knowing this for sure because the recipe is so good it's gone in a flash.

14-ounce package of oyster crackers
1 package Hidden Valley® The Original Ranch® dry dressing mix
    (*this is not the dip mix*)
½ cup oil
1 teaspoon garlic powder
½ teaspoon dill weed
Several dashes Cayenne pepper, to taste

1. Mix oil, dry dressing, garlic powder, dill, etc. in a large bowl.
2. Add oyster crackers and stir.
3. Do not bake. Just stir occasionally. Put in covered container and store.

INSANELY RICH COOKIES

My son's absolute favorite cookie recipe.

Because this recipe uses mayonnaise, I have never tried to freeze the dough. I just bake the whole batch and share it.

1 box Butter Pecan Cake Mix (*Betty Crocker® makes it and I have found it at Walmart*)

2 boxes butterscotch instant pudding mix, the 4-serving size (you can substitute vanilla instant pudding, if you prefer)

1 cup Bisquick®

1 cup coarsely chopped pecans

1 cup chocolate chips

$1^1/_3$ cup mayonnaise

1. Combine all dry ingredients in a large mixing bowl.
2. Add mayonnaise and blend.
3. Drop by spoonfuls onto a greased cookie sheet.
4. Bake at 350° for 12 minutes.
5. Allow to cool on the cookie sheet for 10-15 minutes or they will fall apart.

HAWAIIAN BREAKFAST

1 package sausage patties
1 can pineapple rings in pineapple juice
2 or 3 bananas sliced lengthwise, banana split style
2 tablespoons butter

Cook sausage patties according to directions.

In a separate pan, melt butter over medium-high heat and sauté pineapple rings until the sugars caramelize and they are golden brown. Remove from pan and set aside.

Sauté bananas until tender.

Top sausage with pineapple ring and banana slices.

BRUNCH-ABLE CHEESE PUFF

16 slices dense white bread (e.g. Arnold® Brick Oven White)
Butter, softened
1 (8-ounce) package extra sharp cheddar cheese
6 eggs, well beaten
1 quart of milk
Dash of Worcestershire sauce
1 teaspoon salt
½ teaspoon Dijon mustard
3 strips bacon
Parmesan cheese
currant or guava jelly

1. Trim crusts from bread and butter each slice.
2. Arrange 8 slices, buttered side down, in bottom of well-buttered rectangular baking dish (3-quart). Cover with grated sharp cheese and top with remaining slices of bread, buttered side up.
3. Mix eggs, milk, mustard, and Worcestershire, and pour over bread.
4. Cover and refrigerate overnight.
5. Before cooking, sprinkle Parmesan on top. Bake in a water bath, 350° for about 1 hour or until puffed and brown. Sprinkle with crumbled bacon. Serve with jelly.

(Before assembling this dish, find another baking pan and make sure your 3-quart baking dish will fit inside with enough room to pour a couple of cups of hot water in without spilling over the sides. This will be your water bath.)

BEER BREAD

I know it seems like blasphemy, but this is a great recipe to make with kids because it is so easy and foolproof. Of course, the alcohol bakes off.

1 (12-ounce) bottle or can of beer
$^1/_3$ cup sugar
3 cups self-rising flour

1. Whisk together the sugar and the flour.
2. Gently stir in the beer (it will foam up, which is kind of fun).
3. Pour batter into buttered or sprayed loaf pan.
4. Bake at 350 ° for 1 hour.
5. Serve hot (maybe with some honey butter).

CARPENTER FAMILY SANDWICHES

The first time my mother-in-law made this for me, she was nursing me back to health after I came down with a severe bout of bronchitis. When she brought me the sandwich, my first thought was, *"How am I going to swallow this creation?"* I ended up asking for a second sandwich.

It has an absolutely delicious combination of sweet and savory with a decided crunch from the lettuce, bacon, and peanut butter. (Just so you know, I also like tuna sandwiches made with wasabi mayonnaise.)

If nothing else, I hope it serves as inspiration for your own family sandwich.

1. Toast two slices of white bread.
2. Spread one slice with crunchy peanut butter.
3. Add a layer of crispy bacon over the peanut butter.
4. Top the bacon with a leaf of iceberg lettuce.
5. Finish with a healthy drizzle of Catalina salad dressing (*the original recipe calls for 1890 French dressing, but I haven't been able to find this for years*).

GARCIA FAMILY FRIED EGGS & RICE

Growing up, comfort food always started with rice. This was the go-to dish when we were feeling under the weather. It was simply a bowl of hot, white rice topped with two fried eggs that had been cooked in butter. I have since learned that eggs are the most easily digestible source of protein, so this isn't a bad way to go for a tender tummy or even a quick, no-brainer dinner.

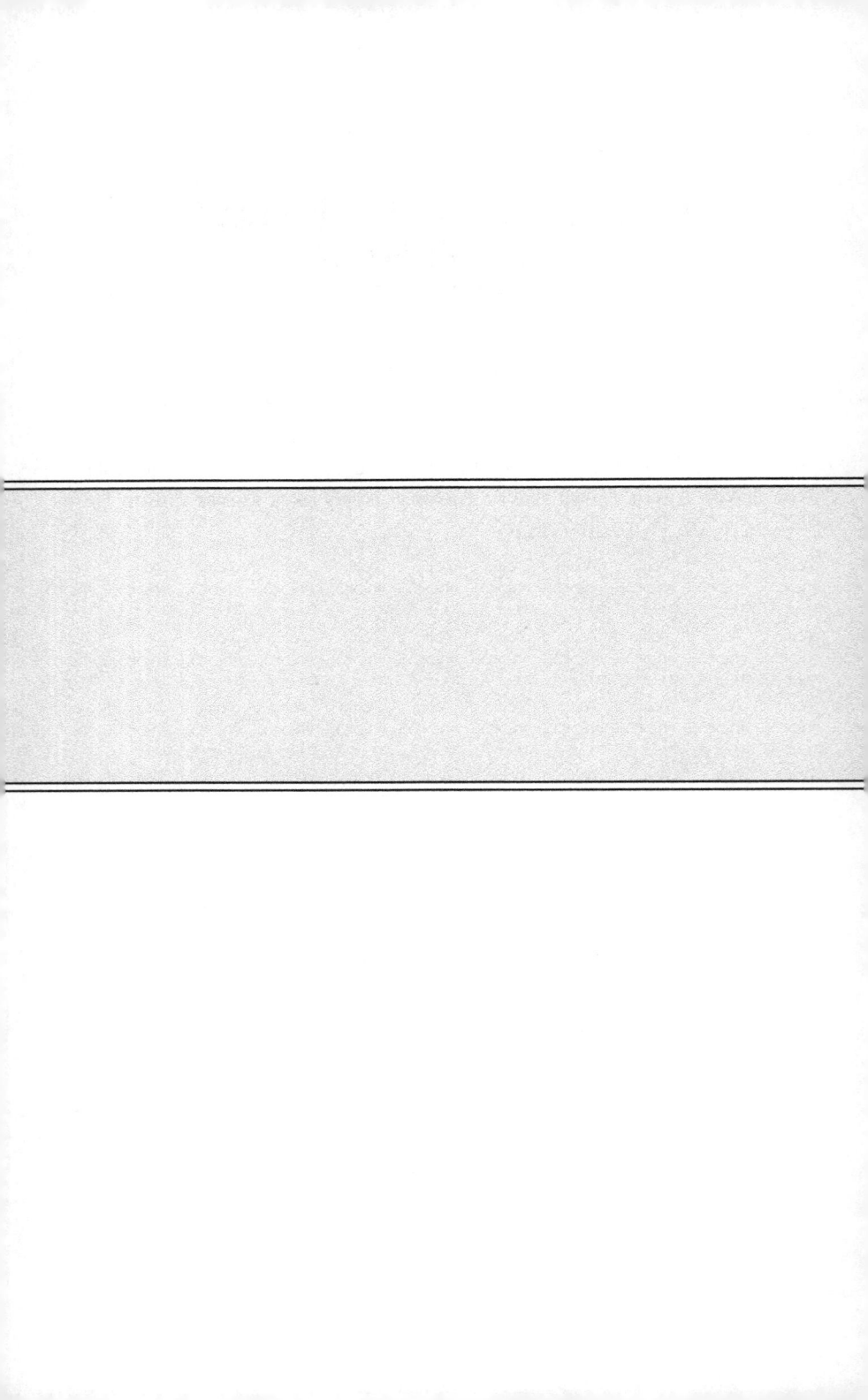

THE FINAL CAVEAT

THE MEASURE OF VICTORY

For Domestic Commandos, attitude often is our chief weapon to successfully make it through the day. It inspires us to address the details that improve our day-to-day lives for our families and helps us to disavow the critical eyes of those who believe we don't meet some politically correct standard they have set.

But attitude is not the key to a happy family.

Laughter is.

Laugh with your spouse, laugh with your children, laugh with your family, laugh with your friends. In fact, the best memories usually involve laughter.

Laughter is the foundation of a life well-lived and a family well-raised.

This is what being a Domestic Commando really is all about.

Roger that!

INDEX

traditions, 70, 71
truffles. *See* chocolate truffles
Turkey Tetrazzini, 153

U

unexpected guests, 89

W

wax paper, 138, 146, 147
working world, 53
wrapping pack, 124
Wrist Buddy, 61